Praise for *Turning Ourselves Inside Out*

"Daye and Fennell offer an outspoken, yet compassionate and wise map for this autumnal season of mainline, white Protestantism in North America. Discerning the 'sacred [in] the deep humbling of the liberal church,' they commend strategies of kenotic descent, community listening, and opening sanctuaries to the streets. From case studies they distill six key virtues for post-Christendom ecclesial leadership, and most importantly point to enduring underground 'mycelia'—'the deep teachings and practices of our tradition . . . carrying nutrients and intelligence for the church.'"

—Ched Myers, author of *Who Will Roll Away the Stone?
Discipleship Queries for First World Christians*

"I love the work of these authors'. We have all heard the reports of decline so often that the trend seems irreversible, even overwhelming. These authors show anew that the God of resurrection is not stumped by death—and that's precisely when resurrection can take place. Fennell and Daye are those rare, brave scholars willing to listen to and learn from lay people. May their tribe increase."

—Jason Byassee, teacher of preaching at the Vancouver School
of Theology and author, with Andria Irwin, of
Following: Embodied Discipleship in a Digital Age

"Why lie down and die when you can go on a journey of self-discovery? This book is not a program, not a litany of how-tos, but an invitation to liberal Christians to engage in a spiritual adventure. Daye and Fennell summon congregations to explore ancient virtues, character traits that have assisted faith communities to find the life and vocation even in a challenging culture."

—Sandra Beardsall, professor of church history and ecumenics,
St. Andrew's College, Saskatoon, Canada, and coauthor of
*Daring to Share: Multi-Denominational Congregations
in the United States and Canada*

"This is a pump *and* well kind of book. Some books help us learn about how the pump works: effective leadership and dynamic mission strategy. Some books help us learn about what's in the well: brave faith and living spirituality. This book does both by taking us to thriving congregations where mission has tapped into deep sources of vitality. In the process, Daye and Fennell uncover virtues that are unsettling, energizing, and ultimately nourishing. This insightful study offers hope to us strugglers who suspect that the pump may have lost connection to the well."

—Peter Short, writer and former moderator of The United Church of Canada

Turning Ourselves Inside Out

Turning Ourselves Inside Out

THRIVING CHRISTIAN COMMUNITIES

Russell Daye and Robert C. Fennell

FORTRESS PRESS

MINNEAPOLIS

TURNING OURSELVES INSIDE OUT
Thriving Christian Communities

Unless otherwise cited, the Scripture quotations are from New Revised Standard
Version Bible, copyright © 1989 National Council of the Churches of Christ in the
United States of America. Used by permission. All rights reserved worldwide.

Scripture quotations marked (CSB) have been taken from the Christian Standard
Bible®, Copyright © 2017 by Holman Bible Publishers. Used by permission.
Christian Standard Bible® and CSB® are federally registered trademarks of Holman
Bible Publishers.

Scripture quotations marked *The Message* are taken from THE MESSAGE,
copyright © 1993, 2002, 2018 by Eugene H. Peterson. Used by permission of
NavPress, represented by Tyndale House Publishers. All rights reserved.

Scripture quotations taken from the (NASB®) New American Standard Bible®,
Copyright © 1960, 1971, 1977, 1995, 2020 by The Lockman Foundation. Used by
permission. All rights reserved. www.lockman.org

Cover image: Phukhanh / IStock
Cover design: Marti Naughton (sMart desigN)

Print ISBN: 978-1-5064-7002-3
eBook ISBN: 978-1-5064-7003-0

CONTENTS

INTRODUCTION
Get Going!

We don't know what we don't know until we discover it. And the path to that understanding is rarely straightforward.

The journey toward this book has been interrupted many times. Life and the work of the Holy Spirit are just like that, don't you find? Our journey of research and writing, listening, and discovering has been winding, disorienting, and confusing at times, but it also has been rich, nourishing, and transformative. Along the way, we have met many inspiring people of faith, both leaders and followers, and have learned much about new forms that Christian faith communities are taking in the twenty-first century as so many traditionally shaped congregations die off. Even while one congregation after another shuts its doors for good, our journey has brought us face to face with inspiration and hope, moments of amazement and insight.

The Thriving Christian Communities Project started in 2015. In many ways, the inspiration for this book came from a Facebook conversation in which someone asked, "We always hear about the problems in our churches. When are we going to talk about the good news stories?" Indeed, in the mainline church, we have been singing the song of decline and despair for so long, we can even harmonize with it.[1] So this got us thinking, How do we learn about what is exciting and what the Holy Spirit is doing? How do we broaden the conversation beyond how sad, afraid, and grumpy we often are as church people? When do we take to heart the psalmist's advice to "sing a new song to the Lord" (Ps 96:1 CSB)? These kinds of questions filled our imaginations when we were scouting out the long walking route of Camino Nova Scotia, the pilgrimage program offered by Atlantic School of Theology. The long hours of walking together gave us the space and peace to think more broadly about what we wanted to learn and how to share it with the wider church. Talking about it made us curious and excited. The spark caught flame, and we took off on this project of discovering and describing thriving local communities of faith. We knew one key thing: we had to go where good things were happening and ask people to tell us in their own words about their experiences of thriving.

So we went out to meet and reflect on Christian communities that were not caught in the death grip that is so pervasive today. We wanted to experience and hear from churches that are finding ways to live in joy, strength, faith, and service. We knew of a few of these and heard rumors of others. The financial support of the Rowntree Scholarship from the United Church of Canada Foundation made it possible for us to travel and meet these folks in person. From the start, our goals were ambitious. We wanted to help others see and imagine where the Holy Spirit is renewing the Christian movement. As Christendom dies, and in the freedom that follows, we have come to realize that we also need to learn how Christianity is being reborn in a heterogeneous array of communities. We wanted to get up close to that diversity—as best we could—to collect and share wisdom, like building a seed bank. We hoped that you, as a reader, would find hope and inspiration and then feel daring enough to plant a few seeds in your own setting.

We had to be aware of our biases too. We made some assumptions. We assumed that the good work of our gracious God is unstoppable. Even when the mainline church declines as a total body, God is still at work in the world. That divine movement can be discerned if we stop to notice and take off our blinders. We assumed that the good news of Jesus Christ and the transforming power of the Holy Spirit are finding outlets and joyful expressions all over the place; we just had to open our eyes and ears. We were aware of our privilege as white, Anglo-Celtic ministers and scholars with advanced degrees, many years of professional experience, and an established institutional base. We hoped that our privilege would not get in the way of our openness to learning or prevent us from seeing what could be seen. We knew ourselves to be people who like to have "grand theories of everything," and we had to try to set aside what we thought we knew about church before we started our research. The people we would interview were the experts, not us. We knew ourselves to be tempted to think we already had things figured out. But we had to go in with what some call "beginner's mind." In the years in which we undertook this study, we have become more and more aware of how personally transformative it is for us to listen to and learn from persons in marginalized and racialized communities. The racism, classism, and sexism embedded in us through our upbringing and the dominant cultural voices we have absorbed for decades are slow to loosen their grip on our imaginations. But we hope for the grace to continue to be learners and to be transformed by those who are unlike us.

METHODOLOGY

How did this research take place? First, we identified a series of Christian faith communities that we knew to be either thriving or revitalizing. All are within the Protestant mainline or liberal tradition, and most (but not all) are congregations. Many of these communities are vital in terms of traditional measures like membership, worship attendance, or participation in programs and ministries. Others were vital in different ways: embracing dynamic spiritual practice, providing gutsy service to the poor, offering a ministry online, or even selling their property and moving out to offer their money and their energy to mission in the larger community. After identifying a list of faith communities in eastern, central, and western Canada, we expanded our list by working with personal contacts to identify communities we had not heard of. Some of these were rural; most were urban or suburban. Our contacts and conversation partners also helped us identify a number of faith communities on the West Coast of the United States. Our focus extended there because this region is living a post-Christian reality similar to that of the Canadian context. To find more research sites, we hung out a shingle on social media and a modest website to ask for thriving faith communities to self-nominate. We also bought some classified advertising space in a denominational magazine, asking for ideas. In the end, we had about sixty communities on our list, but we were able to interview only about thirty-five in person due to time and cost restraints. Later in the process, we interviewed a number of insightful observers and leaders of the contemporary church to test our insights and see what we were missing.

When visiting a "thriving" Christian community, we carried out focus groups with five to ten members. We also interviewed leaders, usually individually but occasionally in clusters of two or three. To gather the data, we relied on in-person interviews and didn't use surveys.[2] Everyone we interviewed signed an agreement to participate that gave them the freedom to withdraw from our study at any time. We started out with a series of questions for the interviews and sometimes modified them as we learned more. We often let our instincts and intuitions guide us. Once in a while, we sojourned for a time with the community to observe its life and to get a feel for the place. When such documents were available, we took home literature about the community to be reviewed later. Over a period of about four years, we talked to each other about once every three months to discuss our field visits (some of which we did together, and quite a bit of it we did separately) and the discoveries they yielded. As we checked in and compared notes, themes and insights came into greater focus. Overall, we focused on the stories that people told us—illustrations and examples of their life together as people of faith. We didn't give as much attention to published studies or theories and in fact only looked at such literature after our field research was complete. When we wrote about the people we met and the places we visited, we changed all the names to keep their identities anonymous. In a couple of cases, we created an amalgamated narrative by combining stories when there were strong similarities between two or three communities of faith.

Formally speaking, this project was a phenomenological study, meaning that we talked to people about their actual experience in the settings where they experienced it. We didn't start with a theory or a model and then try to make the data fit. We didn't even define the term *thriving* in advance, even though it was right in the title of our project and even when people asked us to tell them what we meant by it. The only consideration that we explicitly excluded was *numbers*. We didn't want to know about or measure worship attendance or budgets. We wanted to get behind the numbers to the juicy stuff, the Holy Spirit stuff, that we believe is more important than anything that can be quantified.

SO WHAT?

In the midst of great upheaval, Christ is giving us a new church; we want to give you a glimpse of it. As noted above, the journey of our research and writing was often interrupted because both of us have other jobs. Rob is a full-time dean and professor at a theological university. Russ is a full-time congregational minister, a part-time university lecturer, and an occasional consultant for congregations seeking to revitalize. But looking in the rearview mirror, we see that our day jobs were not interruptions at all. Things we were learning about church and gospel in our academic and congregational settings (and have been learning in such places for more than twenty-five years) were being interwoven with the things we were discovering in the research. All of that learning has produced a *gestalt*—a total picture—that we now present to you in this book.

After collecting most of our data and writing early drafts of the book's chapters, we brought together a small group of Christian leaders whom we admired to workshop the data and the drafts. We asked these trusted colleagues to gather with us on retreat to give us their feedback and critiques. Their feedback was bracing. They told us, "You are holding back. You are pulling your punches, and the heart of the book is buried under a layer of reticence." We were a little shocked but knew they were right. We went back and revised what we had written, then revised it again.

So what was the layer of reticence? Why were we pulling our punches? The answer had to do with anger. Both of us are frustrated and upset about the condition and culture of the mainline church. We take the presence of Christ's mission in our world seriously and believe that a healthy, thriving church is something worth fighting for. But when we look at the mainline church, we don't see a lot of health, courage, imagination, or even faith, to be frank. These things are there to be found if you look hard enough, and you'll hear about them throughout this book, but courageous, imaginative, faith-filled churches are gradually becoming the exception. These frustrations are not unique to us; they are widely shared, often by the leaders we interviewed for this research and among many of our other colleagues and lay folks we know. Christ is alive among us, so many of us can feel the Spirit offering energy and imagination! But we get angry when so many churches and leaders choose eventual death over the risk-taking that comes with being reignited by the Divine. We in the mainline church tend to drift slowly, inexorably toward death and decline, even though deep in our hearts we want the opposite. We want renewal and excitement and to embrace the amazing things God can do! Yet the tepid, hesitant reluctance that predominates in mainline church culture (the culture that formed us and in which we are fully embedded) is killing us off, one congregation at a time. As ministers and scholars and followers of Jesus, that's just not good enough for us. We want better for the church God loves, the church God has chosen to fulfill Christ's mission in the world. We are hungry for more. *What about you?*

HOW TO USE THIS BOOK

What we have to offer in this book is not a series of suggestions for programming, evangelization, or leadership development, but rather a description of a series of character traits, of *qualities*, that both reflect and shape faith communities that are thriving or revitalizing. Our recommendation is that churches that desire to revitalize try to stimulate these qualities in their own settings. Or, to put it in a better way, we encourage you to become vulnerable to the Holy Spirit and invite the Divine to stimulate those qualities in them. We don't want you to imitate these other churches. We want you to overhear our conversations and reflections with them and ask yourselves, What can we do and be in our place? Where is God leading us? What is the beautiful risk we can take for the sake of the world God loves?

How does a community cultivate a character trait? We will have ideas for this in the following chapters, but our first and most important suggestion is to immerse yourself in the stories of faith communities that embody those traits, both those we explore here and others that you come across. There is something organic about the cultivation of character traits. You may read about a program in one of these faith communities that would work in your own. That's good. But even better is to feel your way deeply into the stories of these communities such that you gather a kind of seed. When that seed is planted in your own community, it may grow to produce something that looks quite different. This work will involve deep immersion in your own faith community's story, your local context, history, and promise. Each faith community has its own character, its own soul, its own logic, its own context. The best kind of transformation has organic connections to these things.

We're not offering you an "off-the-shelf" program or model. We're asking you to listen to others' experiences and then dig deep into your own and get down to the business of dreaming God's dream and making it real, right where you are. There is no wrong way to do this—no attempt too small or modest. There is only the faith God awakens in you and the power of the Holy Spirit to spark the flame that will light the way. The rest will unfold as it should.

When we started our research, we did not know if the communities we were going to study would have anything in common. Would they have similar worship styles? Leadership styles? Programs? Theologies? Patterns of volunteerism or lay leadership? Social contexts? At first, the commonalities between the faith communities we studied were hard to see. They were very diverse in terms of the variables listed above. Slowly, however, similarities began to emerge as we reviewed our data. Surprisingly, the similarities that emerged looked like *virtues*. They weren't organizational styles or missions or demographics or leadership philosophies; they were *character traits*—exhibited by leaders, by members, and by the faith communities as a whole.

Chapter 1: When the Storms and Fires Come to the Forest. In this chapter, we unfold in greater detail the broad church and cultural conditions in which the mainline or liberal tradition now finds itself. We offer some observations and diagnoses about those conditions.

In chapters 2 through 7, we describe and explore six traits and related virtues exhibited by thriving Christian communities.

Chapter 2: Starting with "Yes!" Every community, like every person, has an internal narrative, a story or cluster of stories that it carries around telling itself who it is. These narratives can be conscious, semiconscious, or preconscious. Thriving faith communities are unusual in how hopeful and affirmative their internal narratives are. They began with a "yes!" to God, to themselves, to their surrounding communities, and to the larger world. We associate this trait with the virtue of **hope**.

Chapter 3: Learning and Spiritual Growth. The virtue of **humility** allows the people we met in this study to embrace lifelong paths of learning. In particular, they are committed to learning about the way of Jesus

Christ and its implications for contemporary life. As a result, they provide their people and the surrounding community with opportunities to be on a journey of continual learning.

Chapter 4: Openhearted Leadership. In postmodern society, our deep mistrust of hierarchy and its abuses has made many of us in the liberal church suspicious of leadership. This is not the case for the faith communities we studied. They champion leadership and work to raise members up to be leaders as they demonstrate the virtue of *love*.

Chapter 5: Willingness to Risk. We associate this character trait with the virtue of *courage*. Courage manifests in many ways: standing up to injustice, holding to one's principles, having a willingness to sacrifice, even dying for what is right. Here we focus on one aspect of courage: these faith communities stand out in terms of their willingness to take risks—with their property, their theology, their historical identity, their time and energy, and yes, with their money.

Chapter 6: A Sense of Identity. We associate this trait with the virtue of *integrity*. Integrity is usually thought of as an ethical quality, and that is relevant here, but our focus is more on another definition of integrity: being integrated. The thriving Christian communities we examined are marked by a holistic quality in which the various parts of community life—worship, spiritual practice, justice pursuits, leadership styles, and so on—connected organically and reinforced each other. The people of these communities know who they are and why they do what they do.

Chapter 7: Willingness to Be Turned Inside Out. We call this the virtue of *kenosis*. This character trait is hard to describe. It's a little like mercury. It slips from one's grasp. Church after church that we studied had a moment or a series of moments, however, when its doors were torn off and its windows flung open and the world outside rushed in, changing how it lived. These folks realized afresh that the church exists for the sake of the world, and they became eager to serve and love their neighbors in new ways.

At the end of each chapter, there are three questions for discussion and two challenges. We hope that you will consider discussing these and enacting them with a small group from your faith community. We conclude the book with an afterword, asking a final question: Will mainline congregations and parishes become supernovas or black holes?

ACKNOWLEDGMENTS

First, we'd like to thank all the congregations, communities, and ministry leaders we met and learned from. They have been wonderful guides and mentors to us. Their faith and witness have been incredibly inspiring. We also thank St. Andrew's United Church, Halifax, and Atlantic School of Theology for their support for and interest in our research.

Our research assistants and transcribers—Kim Curlett, Dexter Fennell, Sarah Layman, Daniel MacDonald, and Lesley Parsons—have been a huge help. Thank you. We're especially grateful to the United Church of Canada Foundation for providing vital financial support through the Rowntree Scholarship. Pine Hill Divinity Hall also graciously provided financial support for research assistance. Without these grants, this project would not have been possible.

Many colleagues helped us think through the issues and possibilities discussed in this book at various stages, and we thank them: Sandra Beardsall, Rob Dalgleish, Cheryl Jourdain, Ross Lockhart, Catherine MacLean, John Pentland, Chris Pullenayegem, Paul Scott, Peter Short, Michelle Slater, and Kim Uyede-Kai, among others.

Last but not least, we thank our spouses and families, whose patience, love, and encouragement have meant so much to us.

WHEN THE STORMS AND FIRES COME TO THE FOREST

To appreciate the power of thriving Christian communities in the mainline context, we have to be honest about the backdrop against which they stand out. We need to see the dominant experience of the mainline church clearly. Such clear seeing can help us shake the negative energy from our souls and toss away the collected baggage. It can free us to be inspired and moved to action by the counternarrative and by churches that shine in the midst of so much shadow.

Some years ago, a department of the United Church of Canada organized a consultation on the future directions of the church. A senior executive from a large bank was at this consultation and asked about the collective value of all United Church of Canada property, including the thousands of local church buildings around the country. When she received the answer and learned that the figure added up to billions of dollars, she responded, "Well, I know your problem: You don't believe in your mission." Her implication was that if United Church of Canada people really believed in their mission, they would liberate much of that money to support renewal and innovation. She's right. How can it be that the mainline has become stuck in this way? The financial assets frozen in so many emptying buildings are like a quantifiable manifestation of our frozenness of spirit. What is going on?

THE FOREST AND ITS FIRES

The forest and forest fires are metaphors that inform this book, for they have given us as authors a way of understanding what is going on. Some time ago, looking for a quiet space to do some writing for this book, Russ rented a cabin at a retreat center in Nova Scotia called Windhorse Farm. One day, Jim Drescher, cofounder of Windhorse, dropped by for a coffee and a chat. He shared the following true story:

> My family has been going camping on the same land in Northwestern Colorado for generations. It is near the north and west forks of the Elk River. In 1997, a windstorm tore through the land, flattening all the trees in a swath of destruction hundreds of yards wide. It was very strange: the boundaries of the destruction were very clearly demarked, and the trees beyond were untouched. That was the first calamity. Most of the wood up there was pine. All the dead pine in this ribbon of dev-astation became a haven for pine beetles, which exploded in number and then spread into the surrounding forests, killing pine all around. That was calamity number two. Of course, all this dead wood made these hills particularly vulnerable to forest fire, and in 2007, there was a great fire that burned over the whole area. Calamity number three.
>
> This area may never come back the way it was, or it may take hun-dreds of years to repopulate with pine as it was before. And some species may take thousands of years. But the forest is coming back. The first species that is starting to thrive is not pine, but aspen, because aspen lives mostly underground. Aspen reproduces from its roots. One can gaze upon whole hills of aspen, covering square miles, and all one sees can be essentially one tree, with the same DNA, because all the trees have sprung from the same root system. While it looked like all the aspens were killed, they were very much alive underground.
>
> What also survived underground and out of sight was the myce-lia. This is the vast system of fungus that lives under a forest, carrying both the intelligence and the nutrients for that forest. As I said, the for-est may not look the same for hundreds of years, if ever, but it will live! The underground ecology of fungus and roots has already spawned remarkable growth. It will continue with its new assortment of species and find its new balance.

Jim then described how he is letting this "forest teaching" shape how he sees the current crisis within the spiritual community of which he has been a part for a half century: the Shambhala Buddhist community. Shambhala had exploded with controversy as multiple accusations of sexual harassment and assault were leveled against its global leader. He doesn't know if Shambhala will ever look the same and isn't sure it should ever look the same. This crisis may give the Shambhala "ecosystem" a chance to renew itself without patriarchy. What Jim does know, however, is that Shambhala will reform and live on in some other way. He has this confidence because of his half century in the mycelium and roots systems of Shambhala, in the deep teachings and practice that carry intelligence and nutrients. He knows that the mycelium is even now sending up shoots of new life.

Acute crises like the Shambhala scandal and chronic crises like the collapses we have seen in mainline-liberal Christianity each have their own kinds of pain and hope, their advantages and disadvantages. In acute crises, the pain is so sharp and the fear so great that the levels of suffering are extreme. But these very same factors provide a powerful motivation to be honest about the problems, seek responses, and deploy all of a community's resources to bring about reformation. Chronic crises involve lower levels of suffering, but the suffering extends over a longer period of time. The pain slowly creeps in, causing the suffering community to contract and constrict the flow of energy. Much of this happens below the level of awareness because of the slow speed and the small increments of change. By the time most people are prepared to admit that there is a crisis, the community's capacity to respond to it has been diminished. But there is also an advantage here. In a long-term chronic crisis, there are usually early perceivers and innovators, prophetic individuals who have been naming the emergency and experimenting with creative responses long before most people were prepared to listen to them. We met some of these early perceivers and innovators as we researched this book.

Today, the crisis in the mainline church is doubly difficult and doubly full of opportunity because it is both chronic and acute. The liberal church has passed through its early windstorms, through the spreading of pine beetles and rot throughout its ecosystem, and has been burned over by what feels like a great cultural forest fire. After a half century of chronic decline, the levels of pain and fear have now become acute. Here is some good news: a significant number of prophetic individuals and faith communities have been functioning like mycelia. They have descended into the deep teachings and practices of our tradition and are carrying nutrients and intelligence for the church. There has been an underground movement of truth telling and experimentation. Faith communities well suited to the realities of the current ecology of religion in our culture have been springing up like aspen. And they are thriving, adapting, springing up from the roots. They are like the pine cones that *require* a forest fire before they can open up and disperse their seeds.[1]

When we are burned down to our roots, a new opportunity emerges. Under the dead branches and various bits and pieces that have become inert—now all burned away—we get to revisit deeply rooted things. There is so much wisdom, power, insight, and hope buried in the Christian myce-lia. There is the courage of the early churches that faced authorities vio-lently hostile to them. There is the genius of the early evangelists, like Paul, who learned how to articulate the gospel in the language of the cultures through which they passed. There is the diversity of our first centuries as churches grew organically in places like Palestine, Syria, Greece, Asia Minor, Rome, Ethiopia, Egypt, and Libya, taking myriad forms. Ancient spiritual practices were honed in these churches and the monasteries that they birthed. There is the otherworldly insight of mystics like Teresa of Avila and Meister Eckhart, the empathy and honesty of Francis of Assisi. There is the brilliance of our theologians, each finding a way to use the intellectual models of their time, who have carried on an uninterrupted conversation from Augustine to Aquinas to Luther to Schleiermacher to Barth to Bonhoeffer to Tillich to Day to Moltmann to Gutiérrez to Cone to Ruether to McFague to Sugirtharajah to Kwok. There is the inseparable entanglement of prayer and protest that empowered Dr. Martin Luther King Jr. and other civil rights leaders. And there are the gospel encounters of non-Christians like Gandhi, who was so inspired by the Sermon on the Mount.

All the nourishment and genius of this heritage awaits churches that will dig down through the deadwood and ashes of institutional reli-gion. Indeed, the existential ground of Christ's presence, the Community of Heaven, which is both formless and capable of taking infinite forms, awaits them.[2] In the following chapters, we will sojourn with faith commu-nities and leaders who have revisited Christianity's deep things. With the nutrients and the intelligence they have found there, these communities have fostered real vitality in the church, and they are spreading their roots, transforming our underground ecology so that new life may spring up in the contemporary ecosystem of religion and spirituality. They are surprising us by living and finding new ways to live. Death and decline are not their inevitable identity.

But let's stay for a moment with the windstorms, infestations, and fires that have burned over most of the mainline church. An honest look at the scorched earth is needed to understand the challenges innovative churches face in this time and is required for us to know the context in which the genius of the Christian mycelia will have to be applied.

THE DRIVE TOWARD DEATH

Sigmund Freud, in his influential work *Beyond the Pleasure Principle*, identified a "death instinct" or "death drive" in the human psyche.[3] Earlier in his career, Freud had identified a powerful "life drive," which he called Eros. He saw this fundamental life force working in human creativity, reproduction, and vocation. Later, working with patients who had suffered traumatic experiences, he witnessed them returning over and over again to those experiences, causing themselves great pain. Freud's followers came to name the death drive Thanatos. Thanatos also can be a force in patients who have repressed painful experiences. This repression fosters what Freud called a "pressure towards death."

We believe that the mainline church today has its own form of Thanatos. It is a death drive that makes the church toxic and unappealing to the wider society of the United States and Canada. It hastens decline. We see Thanatos played out in church decision-making bodies that exhaust themselves fighting about issues of secondary importance. We see it in congregations that use their last resources clinging to old ways for tiny remnants instead of risking new ways of living the faith. We see it in the resentment directed toward the counterexample churches that actually do find a way to thrive in these hard times. It's true: when a congregation is doing well and finding new ways to thrive, sometimes other congregations get snippy and envious, bad-mouthing their siblings in Christ who are just trying to be as faithful as they can. Why is it so hard for us to celebrate and give thanks for the fresh energy they bring? Thanatos is an energy that underlies the negativity.

Even those churches that have things to celebrate and can offer a narrative of affirmation find it hard to do so because they float in the sea of the larger, toxic, Thanatos-consumed church. They fear the day when the poison waters will lap at their shores.

This is a painful time for the mainline church. There is so much grief. There are so many empty pews. When you visit almost any congregation today, you are more likely to hear a story of loss or complaint than one of faith or mission. How many times have you heard (or said) sentences that begin like this?

> *"I remember a time when . . ."*
> *"Young people just don't . . ."*
> *"I don't know how much longer . . ."*
> *"We've already tried that, and it didn't work . . ."*

The decline of the Christian church is well documented.[4] It has been hashed out in church councils and colleges ad nauseam—sometimes even literally to the point of nausea. This decline has advanced to a stage at which it has become an active, self-strengthening force. Freud's diagnosis of the "death drive" is paradoxically alive and well. There is an expression: "Energy follows attention." We become that upon which we focus. When we become obsessed with what's wrong, we become part of what's wrong. We have trouble seeing anything else.

THE CHALLENGE OF SCIENTIFIC MATERIALISM

There are many reasons for the growth of this death drive. Rejection by a materialist culture that seems to embody so many values antithetical to the gospel makes liberal Christians wonder if their spiritual expressions really are irremediably flawed. The society around us seems to value rationalized leadership and to suspect charismatic leadership—leadership that is itself led by the gifts of the Holy Spirit. We seem to have too few successes in our social gospel campaigns and our efforts toward social transformation. The empirical spirit of the age wants "results" and statistics, but the soul work of faithful Christians doesn't lend itself easily to such a paradigm. And there is more we could say on this. But we have come to see two great causes for the growth of Thanatos standing out above the others. We believe that renewal stands a much better chance if we look these two causes squarely in the eye and confront them. They are, first, a surrender to the scientific materialist worldview of Western society and, second, a guilt-laden denial concerning our role in colonialism. Let's take a brief look at each of these—not to wallow in them but to see our sickness clearly so that we can find strong medicine in the stories of hope that fill the remaining pages of this book. The future of what we once called mainline churches may depend on finding this medicine and healing ourselves, and welcoming the Spirit's healing, from what looks more and more like two serious errors, or even apostasies.

The book *Beyond Physicalism* opens with these words:

The rise of modern science has brought with it increasing acceptance among intellectual elites of a picture of reality that conflicts sharply both with everyday human experience and with beliefs widely shared among the world's great cultural traditions. A particularly stark but influential early statement of the emerging picture came from philosopher Bertrand Russell: "That Man is the product of causes which had no prevision of the end they were achieving; that his origin, his growth, his hopes and fears, his loves and beliefs, are but the outcome of accidental collocations of atoms; that no fire, no heroism, no intensity of thought and feeling, can preserve an individual life beyond the grave; that all the labors of the ages, all the devotion, all the inspiration, all the noonday brightness of human genius, are destined to extinction in the vast death of the solar system, and the whole temple of Man's achievements must inevitably be buried beneath the debris of a universe in ruins—all these things, if not quite beyond dispute, are yet so nearly certain, that no philosophy which rejects them can hope to stand. . . ." There can be no doubt that this bleak vision continues to dominate mainstream scientific thinking and has contributed to the "disenchantment" of the modern world with all its multifarious attendant ills.[5]

This worldview, which is sometimes called physicalism, scientific realism, or scientific materialism, has come to dominate the educational and cultural institutions of Europe and North America and is rising in its impact on other parts of the world. It also has come to dominate the main-line church, even if we pretend otherwise. A good exercise for anyone who wants to gain insight into the extent to which the mainline church has absorbed the worldview of scientific materialism and allowed "disenchant-ment" to creep in is to spend some time with a charismatic or Pentecostal church. Recently Russ was doing that, as an independently networked char-ismatic church[6] has moved into the building owned by the congregation he served, sharing the space. This charismatic church is made up mostly of immigrants from Africa and the Caribbean. Joining them for worship, one is struck by the amount of prayer and the intensity of prayer, as well as both the content and tenor of the preaching and of the singing. Lead-ers and worshippers demonstrate a *passionate* belief that God is an active agent in their lives! God is not some theoretical entity that may in some subtle way be watching and imperceptibly influencing events in the world, which seems to be the most common depiction of divine agency one will hear in most mainline churches today. Members of this charismatic church show up with a palpable hunger for encounter with the Spirit and are open to having their lives melted down and remolded by that encounter. They *earnestly* believe that their hurts can be healed and that healing often actu-ally occurs. They believe that they will be given energy to live the often-challenging lives of immigrants, and they are energized. They believe that money will flow into their church (and its overseas mission projects), and it does. They believe that they will grow, and they do. This congregation has grown tenfold in the last decade. The pastor of this church has a PhD in engineering, and many members have postsecondary education. They have spent time in educational institutions that propagate the worldview of scientific materialism, but they have not *internalized* that worldview. They don't allow it to define for them the possibility or impossibility of a God who can be active in their lives. They don't seem ashamed of their own worldview, even when moving through social spaces shaped by the cultural assumptions of materialism.

In contrast, more and more, the common experience of the mainline church appears to be the opposite of this on every point. Our ministers have been educated in universities where scientific materialism dominates and are often trained in seminaries where the faculty also has absorbed the intellectual ethos of the universities that emphasize physicalism. In the teaching they receive, and often in the sermons they preach, there is a reticence to make claims about divine agency. The active power of God is rarely a theme of the liturgy or the sermon. The toxicity of scientific materialism functions like a vaccine against imagination and spirituality. It seems today that it is a grave sin to make a false promise, so we in the mainline steer clear of anything that sounds like an assurance that God will be active in our daily reality. We've internalized Bertrand Russell's assertion that "no philosophy which rejects them [the tenets of materialism] can hope to stand." In short, we are reluctant to believe and to assert the reality of a God who is in fact powerful, active, present, transforming, and inhabiting the lives of individuals and communities.

The consequences of this surrender to scientific materialism are profound. Very few people are interested in joining an organization that is deeply ambivalent about its core purpose. Very few people under the age of sixty are interested in remaining in such an organization. How many organizations can last while attempting to replace their primary purposes (the nurturing of faith and enacting a mission revealed by God) with secondary purposes (providing a social gathering place, for example), even if those secondary purposes are important and attractive? In the mainline, we often cling to our task of advancing social justice, and God's mission and the pursuit of social justice do indeed overlap. But if the church doesn't bring something to the pursuit of justice that isn't already provided by nongovernmental organizations (NGOs) or social enterprises, does the world really need us? Many mainline church members are proud to announce that their church is "friendly," but is that why we exist? To be friendly? Is that it? Something far more nourishing and transformative needs to characterize our faith communities, something Spirit led and mighty. It's hard to think of a Bible verse in which we are commanded to "go out and be friendly."

Another consequence is that congregations are left feeling helpless in the face of church-specific Thanatos. The best medicine for breaking out of this ennui is hope, but such hope requires a trust that *a power greater than ourselves is preparing a future for us.* Do we dare to believe this?

Can we trust that the promises of Jesus Christ are reliable? Without such hope-filled trust, we won't have the courage necessary to descend into the Ground of Being (as Paul Tillich described the reality of God) and reemerge with new pictures of a future and the energy to pursue it. Our roots won't be the resilient roots of the aspen but will simply wither and die when the above-ground trees that we once were are burned away.

If you are a Christian in the mainline, liberal, or progressive traditions, you might be saying to yourself, "But what about the theology and the ethics of the charismatic churches that you are praising here? Are they LGBTQ+ friendly? Do they embrace other faiths? Do they have a mission to speak truth to the powers of this world? What are they doing about climate change?" These are fair and important questions. But they can't insulate us from learning from faith communities that are quite different from us. A key characteristic of many of the thriving Christian communities we examined is that they are "both/and" churches. They appear to have a deeper sense of trust in God's agency than most mainline churches, and they carry a passion for peace and justice that is sometimes missing in charismatic churches. For them, spirituality and social justice have not been set apart as opposing pursuits. In fact, these churches are often marked by freshness in their pursuit of social justice and relationships with marginalized individuals and groups. That freshness allows them to be unlike the many churches on the Christian right that shrink away from relationships with Muslims, atheists, practitioners of Indigenous peoples' spiritualities, and those of other faith traditions. It also allows them to be unlike the many Christians on the left who shrink away from evangelicals and Pentecostals and from enthusiastic affirmations of God's presence and power. They have an openness that allows them to encounter almost everyone without an attitude of suspicion and instead with eyes ready to perceive the good.

THE CHALLENGE OF COLONIALISM

A second great cause of the death drive in the mainline church is the way it relates to its historical complicity in colonialism. People of color, both African American and Indigenous, have pointed out that the most segregated time in our society is Sunday morning. Meditating on this opens a doorway into seeing clearly the shadow side of liberal Protestantism's role in the societies of Canada and the United States.

During the same centuries that United, Methodist, Presbyterian, Lutheran, Unitarian, liberal Baptist, and other Protestant churches (and we would include the Anglican/Episcopalian church here as well) were casting light upon their members with worship, preaching, Christian education, and charity for the poor, they were also casting great shadows through their participation in a vast colonial project that used enslaved labor, stole land from Indigenous peoples, marginalized immigrants (especially brown-skinned and non-Christian ones), suppressed sexual minorities, and legitimized patriarchy. In Canada, the church-run Indian Residential School system (one of the central components of a genocide) is perhaps the starkest example of this. In the United States—and in the colonies that preceded both Canada and the United States—the commonplace practices of enslavement provide an equally horrifying example.

Today both the church and the larger culture are aware of this legacy and of the stink of culpability that lingers on the church because of it. The difference lies in how secular culture and the church are responding. Many people in the surrounding society identify institutional religion with patriarchy, hypocrisy, and abuse, and they stay away in droves. The church is stuck in denial. As Freud pointed out, conscious denial of something that, deep down, we know to be true produces Thanatos, the death drive.

BREAKING AWAY

Mercifully, through the brave voices of feminists, liberation theologians, civil rights leaders, Indigenous Christians, and queer theologians—not to mention the thousands of courageous preachers of all stripes who have spoken truth from our pulpits and often paid a price for it, together with heroic lay leaders—the Holy Spirit has begun to move us out of denial. Yet when we begin to move out of denial, we often become stuck in debilitating guilt that can paralyze us from taking the next step toward embracing life and the generous impulse of giving ourselves to the greater good.

The first phase of dealing with this guilt (with some blessed exceptions) has not been a great success among mainline Christians. Especially on the left of the church, there has been a temptation to wallow in that guilt and even a fetishization of it.[7] We find so many ways to say "no!" to who we are and who we have been but fewer ways to say "yes!" to those who have suffered from our colonial enterprises. Part of the reason for this is that it seems easier to wallow in guilt than to process the shame, move forward, and deploy a strong "yes!" in relation to those who have been harmed. Such a "yes!" makes greater claims on our money, our time, our energy, and our passion. Let us be clear about what we are not saying here. We are not saying that we should minimize or hide from our colonial past or the forms of colonialism that we still carry. We need to continue to work diligently at bringing those forms to the transformational light of day, and we need to repent of them. But we also need to move through self-recrimination to committed service for and with those who have been pushed to the margins, doing so in modes of action to which *they themselves invite us*. Happily, some of the communities we have studied are doing just that. While not denying the injustices of the past, they are living up to their responsibilities with a powerful "yes!" to their mission partnerships.

So there is nothing simple or straightforward about all this. In the mainline-liberal churches, we live with and carry around with us both colonial impulses and the desire for justice. We long for the breaking-through power of the Holy Spirit but also resist its emergence because of the limitations of imagination ingrained within us by scientific materialism. Despair, decline, and the death drive are realities in our midst, and yet the gospel impels us forward and makes us yearn for a new reality. The storms and fires ravage the "forests" of our faith communities, but the subterranean mycelia of heritage and hope are constantly percolating, threatening to erupt at any moment into new and renewed forms of faith, witness, and service. It is these forms that we'll explore now, among Christian communities that have embraced saying "yes!," who have a strong sense of identity, who are willing to take risks, who are committed to learning and spiritual formation, who embrace and encourage leaders, and who are willing to be turned inside out for the sake of the world God loves.

QUESTIONS FOR DISCUSSION

1. Does some form of Thanatos (the death drive) appear in your experiences of church? What does it look like? Feel like?

2. Do you resonate with Jim's story of the forest fire? What do you see in this story that might apply to your faith community or some other aspect of your life?

3. What would it take for a faith community to embrace both open-mindedness (as the liberal tradition strives for) and a belief in a world filled with God's powerful action (as seen in the charismatic tradition)?

TWO CHALLENGES

1. Lead a small group discussion on the two great challenges—scientific materialism and complicity with colonialism—and how they have affected your faith community.

2. Work with members of that small group to articulate a hopeful response to what you discover together.

STARTING WITH "YES!"
The Virtue of Hope

One of the first churches we visited for the Thriving Christian Communities Project was Grace Church. Russ drove the full width of the Rocky Mountains to get there. With a head full of mountain light and beauty, he entered a bustling, wealthy city, got a good night's sleep, then joined Grace Church for a Sunday morning service. As he drove to the church, it became obvious that Grace is located in a trendy, distinct neighborhood. It is a mix of new and old buildings, with many of the latter turned into boutique shops. There are a lot of places to buy good coffee and good wine or practice your yoga vinyasas. There are high-end condos and street people. On Sunday, like every day of the week, there is plenty of foot traffic. This neighborhood seems to move at a more relaxed pace than other parts of this business-driven city.

FIRST IMPRESSIONS

Coming upon the Grace Church building, one sees that it fits this ethos perfectly. The building is older, but a bright, rainbow-colored banner is stretched across an exterior wall. The banner gives a signal of inclusion, softening the architecture of the building, which wouldn't, on its own, give the message that everyone is welcome. People were lingering near the entrance. The first person to speak to Russ was a street person, whom he assumed was panhandling (correct) and would not go inside for the service (incorrect). The second was an elderly, white, friendly woman who wanted to tell Russ about a social justice project she was championing. The third was a young, gender-fluid person whom Russ had known when they attended university in Halifax. Seeing that this was the congregation they chose to join after moving across the country, Russ immediately assumed several things about Grace Church: it would be queer-friendly, it would not have traditional worship, it would have a dynamic mission to marginalized communities, it would have a sense of humor. All of these assumptions proved to be correct.

The sense of humor was evident even before worship started. People found their way to the pews with loads of conversation and laughter on the way. But they weren't settling into homogenous little clusters that signaled to others to "go somewhere else." One got the sense that the sentence "Excuse me, but you are sitting in my seat" doesn't get used at Grace. When Russ found a seat, the people around him were engaging, and they were interested in hearing about this newcomer and why he had chosen to worship there that Sunday.

Steve, the lead minister, walked up front to lead worship wearing jeans, a sport jacket, and a dress shirt open at the neck. It was quickly evident that he would be very comfortable in the area's boutique cafés and wine bars and also with the full assortment of people strolling on the streets outside. And what was true of Steve was true of the worship. It was a mix of old and new. Worship fit like a pair of shoes that were well made, not cheap, but attending to comfort as well as beauty. Sacred and secular music were mixed. Some of the songs easily could have been among those rotating on the playlists in the cafés. Preaching was narrative and personal. The sermon showed that Steve was a good listener who was touched by the stories of the people with whom he had spent time that week. During the fifteen-minute talk, even though he was the only one speaking, it became clear he had that knack for making people feel special. It's a knack that comes from listening with the kind of interest that is only natural for those who truly like other human beings in all their range of strangeness.

Everything offered in the worship by the leaders, several of whom were lay members assigned performance pieces or prayers, was done well. But there was no sense of straining to reach the heights of perfect performance. Instead, there was a confident unveiling of the heart. The place had heart. The preaching and praying had heart. The personal interactions on the way in and out had heart. That Sunday morning, there was a sense that Christ's heart was being revealed along with the heart of the community—and that every heart that had made its way into the sanctuary that day was welcome, even those that contained guilt or shame, bitterness or fear.

Such openness of heart requires another quality that also was present at Grace—*ease*. When Russ settled into the service that morning, he started to notice that something was missing, something that is usually present in mainline churches. In most churches, it's not obvious but lies under the surface: an emotional current of anxiety. These are uneasy times for the liberal church. Denominational offices are anxious, church governing bodies and bishops are anxious, theological colleges are anxious, treasurers are very anxious. This culture of apprehension finds some expression in most congregations. Each one processes it in its own way (or fails to). Some do so creatively, and many miss the mark with unhelpful forms of denial or projection. But some form of emotional strain usually is present.

It was the absence of this strain that Russ noticed. He wondered if he was fooling himself and decided to stay attentive to this through the week as he sojourned with Grace's ministers, church council, and lay leaders. Perhaps the strain was well disguised at worship but would be present in meetings. Over the course of his visit at Grace, Russ became convinced that his initial perception was correct. Of course, Grace has its issues and challenges and its own emotional "field" that includes some negative emotions. That's normal enough. But the broad-based, amped-up anxiety that can be found in many churches just doesn't seem to be there. After analyzing all of the data gathered at Grace Church—from a focus group with lay members, interviews with ministers and other staff, notes taken during a church council meeting, as well as impressions gleaned from simply hanging around for a few days—we saw that these two qualities, emotional ease and openness of heart, are central to Grace Church's well-being. They are at the center of its relationship to the larger community and the larger culture. Emotional ease and openness of heart reflect an underlying virtue of hope that characterizes this community of faith. They are not leaning backward and falling into nostalgia for what once was. They are leaning forward with hopeful expectation about what is to be.

We should pause for a minute and tell you about the growth of this congregation. Yes, there is growth in terms of attendance and budget, but that's not the most important thing. Grace also has experienced growth in terms of the diversity of people who now feel welcome there, the vibrancy of small groups, the range of forms of mission, the web of interfaith friendships, and the variety of emergent lay leaders. The story of Grace Church has a lot to teach us about the crucial nexus where the internal culture of a church and the culture of the larger community intersect. Plenty has been written about the way churches should communicate to the larger community, like the messaging that should be offered and strategies for evangelization. Yet there is something that lies deeper than these tasks: the *emotional system* of a church. When a human being encounters another human being, she looks (consciously but mostly subconsciously) for clues as to the emotional makeup and *underlying character* of that person. Is she honest? Is she enthusiastic about life? Is she authentic? Does she have some underlying emotional dynamics about which I should be careful? What is she signaling about her impression of me? Does she appear to like who I am?

THE "DOUBLE NO"

These same questions come into play when a newcomer comes into contact with a faith community. They are also at play at the points of intersection between a faith community and the larger community. So many churches today (perhaps because of the "death drive" described in chapter 1, as well as the simple fact that our culture is running away from institutional religion) have a twofold emotional dynamic that is a turnoff to those who come into contact with those churches. We'll call this the "double no." The "double no" is palpable even when folks aren't fully aware of it. It is a "no" to what is happening inside the church, like empty pews, strained budget, and the absence of younger generations. It is also a "no" to what is happening outside the church: the flight from traditional religion, materialism, and the predominance of popular culture. This "double no" can make any local church unappealing. It is as if an individual you meet is signaling internal rejection of both himself and you.

An impressive quality of Grace Church is the absence of both sides of the "double no." Grace signals an emphatic "yes!" to itself and to the larger community. There is a constant stream of "yes!" energy to the congregation's internal culture and the larger culture in which it swims. When a cluster of laypeople from Grace gathered for a focus group, this was the first question we asked: "What is the one thing that we need to know about Grace Church in order to understand it?" Here are excerpts from the first four responses to that question:

> I would say the messaging that's given from the pulpit in nonchurch language. Any particular service touches on so many aspects that, no matter where people are coming from and how they're feeling that day, there's something that touches them. It could be a particular music piece—it could be all parts of the sermon. But it's in very receivable language.

> For me, Grace Church is real. It meets people where they are, and it doesn't create church as a vehicle to change that reality into something better or something nicer. . . . I think the nice thing is that, while Grace is affirming and here to be supportive of people, it doesn't try to sugarcoat life or try to make it something life isn't.

> We're not about just following a rule because it's a rule. . . . It's a group of real people who are about authenticity, are about just exploring boundaries that need to be explored. Affirming ministry is a prime example of that, a very explicit example of that. Something that was considered to be condemnable to hell for so long [homosexuality], and all of a sudden our church is saying, "Wait a second, what's really going on here?" As opposed to just saying, "Well this is the way it is." That's indicative to me. That's what I've been seeing in all corners. . . . It's not just about going, "We're just a church and this is how we function."

> What really works for me, and it has consistently since Steve came, is that (and he's said a few things that've been considered radical in a lot of churches) we are of the community. He talks about having the Bible in this hand and the Globe and Mail [newspaper] in the other hand. I love that concept because you can't be divorced from the world. . . . The other thing that is perfect for me, too, is the welcoming aspect.

Steve says virtually every week, in one way or another, that you're fine to come to God just as you are. In many churches, you're not fine to come to God just the way you are, but at this one, you are. At this one, whatever you bring is fine. I love that part.

SO MANY WAYS TO SAY "YES!"

Often, when we lead a focus group with a cluster of members of a church and ask "What is the one thing that we need to know about your church in order to understand it?" we get very diverse answers. This wasn't true with Grace. The interviewees talked about many aspects of the congregation over the course of the discussion, but they were immediately able to identify the key characteristic that makes Grace vital and attractive. "We are *of the community.*" Grace is all about saying "yes!" to the community. "Yes" to sexual minorities. "Yes" to racial diversity. "Yes" to the everyday experiences of individuals, even when those experiences "suck" (as one interviewee put it). "Yes" to those coming through the doors for the first time, even when those folks are street people who need a shower and talk to themselves during the service. "Yes" even when there is someone who looks more buttoned-down and conservative than most folks at Grace. And "yes" is communicated in "receivable language"—the language heard on the streets and in homes and in the wine bars. The constant stream of "yes" messages has created a congregational culture that is hopeful and expectant.

This quality is something that is strangely rare today. Churches on the theological, political, and social right side of the spectrum have a tendency to declare a "no!" to the world because of personal sin. Churches on the left side of the spectrum have a tendency to declare a "no!" to the world because of social sin, even if they avoid using the word *sin.* Many churches do carry an affirmation of the gospel and of God's vision for the world, but they communicate so much frustration with how different the world is from that vision that they mostly become about saying "no." The challenge is to see God at work in the world around us instead of trying to make the world look more like us. Both those on the right and those on the left struggle with this.

You may be thinking, "But—but there is so much bad stuff in the world that needs to be confronted. What about that? Shouldn't the church be proclaiming a great 'no!' to those things?" Of course, it should. That is part of the Christian movement's prophetic task. It should be confronting every form of injustice that it can. But when this confrontation leads to the deep character of the church being shaped much more by a "no" to what is wrong than to a "yes" to what is right—humankind in all its array and potential, creation and creativity in their myriad forms—then the church is neither really living the gospel nor inviting to those who might engage with it. The habitual "no" moves deep into the heart of our congregations and makes us all the more prone to rejecting innovation and creativity. We become naysayers without becoming truth tellers. It's a constant spiral of negativity.

There is a critical nexus where three things meet: the church, the world, and God's mission. Historically, the church has been deeply shaped by the call to be "in the world but not of the world." It has assumed that the world needs God's mission and is only the *receiver* of that mission. It has also assumed that the church uniquely understands, carries, and enacts God's mission. The church, and only the church, is the *deliverer* of that mission. Few mainline ministers or lay leaders actually speak like this anymore, although the idea is deeply embedded in our collective understandings. Many would say, "Of course God is in the world as much as she is in the church," but the actual disposition of congregations and their leaders usually belies having been shaped by this view of things. In Christian faith communities like Grace Church, however, there is a different understanding of the nexus where church, world, and God's mission meet. A couple of comments from focus group participants reflect this:

> I think that a big part of what we're doing, especially being in an area like this neighborhood, where we have a great avenue to reach out to the broader context, is to reclaim church. It's to reclaim the negativity, the harshness, the judgmental language. . . . We can take that language back, and we can make church a part of society again. It doesn't have to come with a negative connotation. It can come with a positive connotation. It can be an embracing, authentic community that says, "We don't know all the answers, but we're in this journey together." I think that is Grace's greatest challenge and opportunity as we continue to grow: How do we embrace the nonchurch world even more than we

are today? Not with the idea that we're going to convert them and save their souls and bring them into church [but] more [with the idea] that we want to be relevant. We want to reclaim all of the negative things that the church has done in the sense of making church be a positive connotation again.

The speaker does not assume that the church is the carrier of God's grace to a larger community that is mostly the recipient. In fact, he can see that such a view has made the church negative, judgmental, and unappealing to the community. In contrast, his hope is not to make the society look more Christian but to "make church a part of society again." Not "make church appealing to society," or "make church attractive to people," but "make church *a part* of society." As he sees it, "the challenge and opportunity" are to weave church into the fabric of the larger community, which is seen as itself a location of God's grace, not God's opponent. A comment from another focus group participant makes it clear that she believes that goodness is to be found in other places and that Grace Church is part of an ecology that connects it to those other places: "One of the things about Grace is . . . that a lot of people have come and gone out of the community. We welcome them when they come, and we don't necessarily like to see people go, but we don't take it as a bad thing. They came for their faith experience, and their faith experience moved them somewhere else. If that's the case, that's the case. I think it's because the community is so diverse that people are allowed to do that."

BECOMING MYCELIA

It may be helpful to recall Jim Drescher's story of forest fires and restoration that we told in chapter 1. Jim recounted the dynamics of a huge forest fire on land he visits every year in Colorado. While the fire left devastation on the *surface* of the land, he was moved by the speed with which the forest began to restore itself, attributing this to the amazing ecology that lives under the surface of the forest, especially the root systems of the trees and the mycelia—the vast ecology of fungi that connects trees and other plants, even across species, and facilitates the sharing of nutrients and intelligence. This is a useful analogy for understanding the critical nexus where the church, the world, and God's mission meet. One can see that Grace Church's understanding is that they are one tree in a broad cultural ecosystem. The congregation's health and vitality lie in deep integration into that ecosystem, in which nourishment and intelligence flow in both directions, into Grace Church and out of Grace Church. Trying to exert control over this flow would be unhealthy. If Grace were to see itself as the dominant species that provided superior nutrition to the other species, the harmony and vitality of its relationship to the ecosystem would break. It would introduce *dis-ease* into that relationship. Similarly, trying to restrict the flow of nutrients to one direction—drawing in resources to support the growth of the congregation but not allowing them to empty out as well—would also introduce dis-ease.

This understanding shapes the way Grace confronts colonialism, systemic racism, homophobia, and other evils in the world. Its preference is to confront these ills together with a diverse array of partners. In confronting Islamophobia, it does so through partnerships built with the Muslim community. In confronting the oppression of Indigenous peoples, it does so in partnership with First Nations. In confronting homophobia, it does so in partnership with the LGBTQ+ community. Their rage at injustice is mixed with the joy of friendship built across the barriers of historical silos. Grace Church's understanding of itself as an integral part of the larger cultural ecology makes it different from so many iterations of Christianity. Too often the church has indeed seen itself as the dominant species, providing the only real spiritual nourishment. In more recent decades, as anxiety over survival took over, the mainline churches often have displayed a parasitic disposition, desperately trying to suck in resources from the larger community without releasing nourishment to support that community.

One sign that Grace Church is different from so many withering and dying congregations is the willingness of its members to go out into the postmodern, organized-religion-rejecting world and happily tell their friends and neighbors that they belong to a church. As one layperson put it,

I have no qualms about talking about my life at Grace with people who are outside of Grace. I'm not talking about other church people here. People ask, "Oh yeah, I know you go to church. Why do you do that?" And I tell them why I go to church. I would have never done that a few

years ago. Now I'm not afraid at all to say, "Well, I go to a church that's
not like church. You should come here. It's not like church." Meaning
that it's not like your traditional church where you go, and you listen
to the choir, you say a few prayers, you have some tea, and go home.
We don't do that here.

Grace Church has created an ethos—it has grown a soul—that thrives
in the contemporary cultural ecology that is all too ready to be contempt-
uous of conventional churches where "you listen to the choir, you say a
few prayers, you have some tea, and go home." One of the beautiful charac-
teristics of that ethos is that it continually resonates with affirmation and
hope. While so many congregations suffer from the "double no," at Grace
one continually encounters a narrative of "yes!" In the days following the
focus group, Russ kept bumping into this "yes." There was an energetic
"yes" to Christian prayer and spiritual practices, "yes" to shared, interfaith
practices, and "yes" to stuff that was a little new age-y. "Yes" to the ambitious idea of providing lunch to the community every Sunday after worship. "Yes" to having their beloved lead minister flit around the country
visiting with other churches, schools, and gatherings to share their story.
"Sure, Steve's great, but he's not the only one around here who can preach a
sermon," as one person put it. He went away on sabbatical, and the church
grew. He loves to tell that story.

This disposition of affirmation and hopeful outlook is maintained
when Grace turns its eyes from its internal dynamics to the dynamics of the
larger community in which it is planted. Without losing sight of the shadow
sides of contemporary culture, Grace has found a way to say "yes" to it: "yes"
to its music, to yoga, to community bike rides, to other faiths. There is a big,
loud "yes" to the LGBTQ+ community, to Black Lives Matter, to atheists, to
conservatives, and to street people and others cast aside by society. It is a
lot easier to invite people when their first impression of you is not that you
judge them and their values.

CHANGING THE CULTURE OF DECISION-MAKING

This overarching disposition toward "yes" has allowed Grace to give significant attention to *opportunity*, with a level of open-mindedness that is rare indeed in the mainline church. Someone comes along and offers to lead a contemplative practice group weekly. This someone is not ordained and doesn't generally practice out of a formally Christian tradition. The congregation says, "Go for it! Let's see what happens." Someone else says, "We have a mission opportunity with the LGBTQ+ community. Let's hire a coordinator." It's clear that the current year's budget has no allocation for such a position. Still, they say, "Go for it! Let's see what happens." Someone looks at the number of hours their lead minister is spending on administrative work, which is neither his strong suit nor what Grace Church folks want him spending his time on, and says, "We need an executive director." Executive directors are *not* a part of this congregation's past and not common in their denomination. But they say, "Go for it! Let's see what happens." This willingness to experiment has led to more than twenty new paid appointments in recent years. Nearly all are part-time, but we're not talking about tiny numbers of hours here. Every year it seems Grace grows beyond its budget and accepts a level of expenditure larger than current financial giving. And every year the community expands to fit its ambition. We don't think that one liberal, mainline church in one hundred would tolerate this level of risk, but it has paid off for Grace Church year after year. It really does live in a world of abundance instead of scarcity. It lives in a world of Spirit-led hope.

So what has been the most important factor in Grace Church's capacity to say "yes" to itself and to the larger community, in its culture of affirmation, in its willingness to experiment, take risks, and pursue opportunity? After reflecting on this congregation, we do not believe it is any of the things congregational development literature frequently focuses on: a specific theology, communication strategies, leadership styles, stewardship work, or anything that we'd imagine at first. These factors are all important, but they are all subsumed in a larger, encompassing dynamic—the emotional "field" of the faith community. Grace has grown an emotional field characterized by hope, courage, trust, honesty, and joy. It has grown an emotional "body" that is covered by these virtues.

THE "ANGEL" OF A CONGREGATION

Another way of speaking about this is to describe Grace Church's emotional body as its collective spirit. Biblical scholar Walter Wink's trilogy on "the Powers" has influenced many Christian preachers and leaders who want to dive into the intersection of spirituality and justice. Taking his cue from the Second Testament[1] writers' depictions of "the Powers," Wink asserts that every human collective—a nation, an institution, a faith community— has a collective character, a communal spirit. He referred to these collective spirits as "angels." There can be the angel of the nation, the angel of the congregation, and so on. These angels have deep character and maintain much of their original nature over years and even centuries as people come and go from these nations or congregations. They shape the actions of these human collectives and their individual members. The angel of any human collective can be transformed, Wink argues, but such transformation requires concerted work in "engaging the Powers" through prayer, truth telling, and other actions.[2]

The vitality of Grace Church arises in no small measure from the fact that its angel embodies a big "yes" in relation to both the larger community *and* the Christian mycelia. This is not just generalized openness to the larger community and culture but also openness to all the power of Christian faith and tradition. One of the great challenges for Christianity today in the United States and Canada is that the majority culture, perceiving the institutional church to be hypocritical and archaic, rejects the intelligence and nutrients that could flow into it from the Christian mycelia. Faith communities like Grace Church, with their freshness of spirit, their playfulness, and their iconoclasm, become points of connection between the Christian mycelia and the surrounding culture with intelligence and nutrition flowing in both directions, giving them a dynamism and a mischievous joy that comes from flaunting both societal and ecclesial assumptions.

Has Grace Church always been blessed with this emotional body? Has its angel always been this playful and affirming? Definitely not. So how did it get to this place? It arose through a time period when it was blessed with the essential qualities of *weakness and vulnerability*. It was a time of death and resurrection. Grace Church's vitality emerged after being weakened by a phenomenon that was common among several of the thriving faith communities we studied: decline, loss, and even near-death experiences. Before hiring Steve, Grace had gone through a long era of decline, with the inevitable grief experiences of loss, denial, anger, and bargaining. Ultimately, this culminated in a kind of surrender. There came a point at which the congregation was able to say, "What the hell—we're almost dead, so let's try doing things differently." One of the things they decided to do differently was to hire a disruptor/innovator. This was Steve, and he was well placed to be a disruptor/innovator because his career as a minister had itself encountered real disruption. For a time, he had left ministry to work as a social entrepreneur. This gave him an unusual freedom from fear of failure, and this in turn shaped his relaxed modus operandi. That open spirit became contagious and an important part of Grace's ability to maintain a sense of ease as they entered a new phase. His time in the world of social innovation also gave him direct experience of the movement of the Spirit outside the institutional church. He knew that God was at work beyond the bricks and mortar of any one congregation's building.

There is a kind of surrender and relaxation at the stage of acceptance. This involves an emotional release that makes altering the emotional field possible. It's as if the "angel" of the congregation relinquishes its hold a little bit and becomes open to having its character transformed. At that moment, a faith community can open itself to experimentation because it feels, "what do we have to lose?" At the very worst, they would crash and burn. But that might happen anyway. In our research, this "low" moment also emerged as a moment of opportunity, often coinciding with the hiring of a minister whose way of doing things is not especially traditional and whom the church may never have chosen before hitting bottom.

THE WAY UP IS DOWN

A minister whom we will call Sam had just such an experience when he was called to an English-speaking church in small-town Quebec. At his interview, he was told, "If you come, you will likely be our last minister. All of the young English people move away from here, and the French people are Catholics." Shortly after Sam's arrival, a young husband-and-wife music team also was hired. They were full of ideas and keen to play music that the longtime churchgoers weren't very fond of but were willing to accept because it brought joy to the service. Before long, a good number of people who certainly weren't regular churchgoers were joining the choir, which grew to about one-third of the Sunday attendance. The pews started to fill with quite an assortment of other "unchurched" people as well.

Soon a cluster of emerging leaders—about a dozen in all, mostly those with little church experience, but also a few former Roman Catholics—were joining the staff in getting up to all kinds of holy mischief. They tried experimental worship, dialogue sermons, coffeehouses, concerts with African American choirs from the United States, a community kitchen for food bank patrons, transforming Bible studies that used drama and play with clay, and multiple children's programs. The old-timers in the church smiled wry smiles, shook their heads, and (with a few exceptions) accepted the changes because it was the most fun and joy the church had known in a long time. Without doing any intentional stewardship work, the church moved financially from the red into the black. Using some of these funds and lots of volunteer sweat, the congregation was able to fix up and paint both the church and the manse after many years of neglect.

We have witnessed this kind of renewal in several nearly dead congregations over the years: some rural, some urban, some suburban. Part of the courage for experimentation in Sam's congregation came from knowing of the amazing renewal in a church in Ontario some years earlier. This happened when a newly ordained minister arrived to find a congregation that was very close to closing its doors. She helped the remnant adopt an attitude of "What the hell, let's experiment." This minister was brave, iconoclastic, and deeply committed to both spiritual practices and justice work. The result of her collaboration with lay innovators has been a very powerful city-center ministry, especially for and with the LGBTQ+ community and other marginalized folks. A key move in this renewal was the flinging open of the church's doors to people who don't usually find a welcome in a church: sexual minorities, street people, the mentally ill, and the poor. The "yes" to these people turned out to be a "yes" to God. It turned out to be a great shout of hope against the shadows of despair and exclusion.

Although that minister moved on long ago, the church continues to live out the ethos and mission born at that time.

This is what Andrea, another iconoclastic minister, had to say about her arrival at Tenth Street Church, an urban congregation in a large city in central Canada:

> When I arrived, they were skeptical about the future or perhaps resigned about it. But they were also a bit of resurrection church in that they had gone through the Good Friday experience and put everything on the table and decided, "Well, I guess that's it; we should just close the doors." The church was almost one hundred years old, and they sort of hoped to live to be a hundred and then close the doors. That was the perspective of the older congregants. "Let's just get to a hundred, and then we can say we had a hundred years." About a year and a half before that, they had lost the minister, and somebody said, "Well, we lost a minister, but we haven't lost a church yet." And that was, I think, a turning point where they actually faced death, and then they started to look for life again. And so they chose a minister who was outside of the box. They said "yes" to almost everything I wanted to try.

Tenth Street Church's numerical growth since that time has been modest, but they are making a name for themselves as a risk-taking, gutsy, and innovative faith community. One of their gutsy moves was giving sanctuary to a family who had been turned down as refugees and was about to be deported from Canada. Tenth Street has become a destination church, and a number of vibrant lay leaders travel across the city to join them for worship and righteous troublemaking.

GETTING THERE FROM HERE

So what about faith communities that are still very much caught up in the vicious cycle of visible decline, attitudes of scarcity, and incapacitating anxiety? Maybe that's an ecosystem you recognize in your context. It is certainly common across the mainline. What can leaders do in congregations that are not ready to surrender and relax? We know so many clergy who work in such congregations—so many. They are faithful and eager for a healthy church ecosystem. They have insight into the dynamics of their congregation and try to point out these dynamics to the membership. But all too rarely does simply verbalizing this insight do any good, even when it is noted repeatedly, faithfully, forcefully, or gently. Rabbi Edwin Friedman, a systems theorist, explains why this doesn't work: "The colossal misunderstanding of our time is the assumption that insight will work with people who are unmotivated to change. Communication does not depend on syntax, or eloquence, or rhetoric, or articulation but on the emotional context in which the message is being heard."[3]

Like individual people, communities can only absorb truths that they are emotionally ready to accept. The work of leaders in communities still stuck in the big "no" is to alter the emotional context. Or, to put it another way, altering the emotional state of the angel of the community. The key move here is *descent*. These faith communities need to move down into the emotions and fears that are frozen at the preconscious level of the communal body.

How can that happen? We suggest extended, transformative conversations. Such encounters, sometimes called "adaptive" conversations, go progressively deeper, give voice to buried emotions, hopes, and fears. They shift attention from problem-solving toward pervasive change in the ethos of the community. Adaptive conversations can provide a deep cultural shift in a community or organization. Unlike technical problem-solving, where the problem or challenge can be precisely defined and clear solutions articulated, adaptive conversations take longer, progress at varying speeds, and are used when an organization knows it needs deep change but isn't clear about the central challenges or problems it faces. There is more than one way to do all this: study groups, sharing circles, and so on. Leaders shouldn't underestimate the time, preparation, courage, and patience that truly transformative conversations require. They are costly in these ways. But the potential for real grace and liberation is incredible. Such conversations move through phases like the following:

- tentative truth telling

- deeper sharing

- lament

- more honest truth telling

- healing and restoration

- opening to new ways of seeing things

- a shared vision for the future

- readiness to strike out with daring into an unknown future

One of the blessings of this kind of process is that the community makes space through which the winds of the Spirit can blow. Once the Spirit starts to move through a congregation or parish, its members open to the agency of the Divine in their midst. While it may only be tentative at first, they start to believe that it is possible that God is actually acting in their lives. This is essential! Hope in what God can do—not just what we can do on our own—is crucial to the conversations and the transformations.

If you are a leader in one of the many congregations short on hope and characterized by an internal "no" in this time, take heart! Start talking to others and dive into some excellent literature. Take heart because a period of real negativity often precedes the rupture that creates space for light, honesty, and renewal. When we say, "start talking to others," we mean two groups of others. The first group is leaders in other faith communities. There will be many experiencing the same things as you are. Just having honest, safe conversations about your experiences—in which a real depth of feeling is shared, not just the common form of complaining that doesn't attend to the underlying pain—will open up space in you and perhaps your church too. Also, start talking honestly with members of your faith community, preferably in an adaptive conversation that is well planned and extends over a good period of time. At the end of this book, in appendix 2, we offer a four-week study and discussion process for faith communities that would like to explore descent, renewal, and reemergence, as well as some suggested resources for communities who would like to do this more deeply and over an extended period of time.

There are wise elders who have pioneered pathways of insight into this work already. Their writing can work as medicine for the spiritual maladies of today's church. We recommend the work of Edwin Friedman, especially *Generation to Generation* and *A Failure of Nerve*, if you would like to explore further the idea of emotional context.[4] Likewise, we recommend the work of Otto Scharmer and his colleagues, especially *Leading from the Emerging Future* and *Theory U*, if you would like to explore the notion of descent and reemergence.[5] Besides Walter Wink's excellent trilogy on "the Powers," we also recommend his *Transforming Bible Study*.[6] Another excellent source for congregational and leadership studies is The Alban Institute (https://www.alban.org), which has produced materials such as Gil Rendle and Alice Mann's *Holy Conversations*.[7] For an extended process of adaptive conversations, see Martha Grace Reese's *Unbinding the Gospel*.[8]

QUESTIONS FOR DISCUSSION

1. What are some ways your faith community carries an internal "yes" and an internal "no"?

2. Describe the character of your faith community's "angel" or its collective personality. You might want to draw or paint this angel.

3. Discuss what we call "the crucial nexus," where the internal culture of a church and the larger culture of the community (and society) of that church intersect. What does that nexus look like for your faith community? Is it a healthy and flourishing nexus, or does it need some attending to?

TWO CHALLENGES

1. Discover Walter Wink's understanding of "the Powers" in his book *The Powers That Be: Theology for a New Millennium*.[9]

2. Create a study group to examine the internal culture and character of your faith community and the ways in which its "angel" may need to be challenged or transformed.

LEARNING AND SPIRITUAL GROWTH
The Virtue of Humility

On a busy Tuesday evening, as you first walk in the "real" entrance of St. Timothy's Parish Church—the back door off the parking lot—you have to pause and look twice. A friendly mob of teenagers is liable to bowl you over as they barrel down the hallway, laughing, to rejoin their youth group in the youth minister's office. Next door in the gym, the enthusiastic camp song of a community Scouting group boils over into incoherent shouting and laughter. One floor up, a lay leader sets out coffee and tea for a book group that is working its way through the latest Brené Brown bestseller. In a few minutes, the group will trickle in and pull up comfy upholstered chairs, cheerfully checking in on their weeks and lives before settling down for a conversation about spirituality and the rest of life. In the church parlor, St. Timothy's priest is just wrapping up a session on baptism for new parents who will bring their children to worship in two weeks to receive this ancient sacrament of blessing, naming, and transforming. The parents who have gathered are sleep-deprived but excited about presenting their children before the community for this special moment. And online—out of sight of everyone—a prayer group is exchanging requests and prayers as they meditate at home (or in coffee shops, airport lounges, or campus library carrels) on the needs of those they know, their church family, and the wide world. If you had come by earlier in the day, you would have met the Bible study group that has met on "Tuesdays at Ten" for over fifteen years. If you drop by tomorrow night, you'll see a different building, this time filled with recovery groups, yoga practitioners, and a group of leaders doing a visioning exercise.

These are images of a thriving Christian community that is also a community of learning and spiritual practice. The drive to learn and grow is written deep into the DNA of St. Timothy's Parish. It has made a serious commitment to be together in these ways. The parish council, the priest, the wardens, and the lay leadership know and trust that the efforts they make at learning are part of a perpetual process of transformation in Christ.

STILL FIGURING IT OUT

St. Timothy's, like many thriving Christian communities, exemplifies the virtue of *humility*. They don't assume in advance that they have everything figured out. They are lifelong learners on a spiritual quest, seeking to love God and learn from the Way of Jesus. Over against a culture that is so fixated on mastery and control (ever since the Enlightenment of the seventeenth century), churches and groups like these are choosing to set aside their pride and say, "We're ready to learn." The ancient notion of being a *disciple* is alive and well in this attitude. A disciple or apprentice is open to being taught, being coached, being led. The virtue of the disciple spirit is humility—staying low and close and open; not vaunting oneself over others; not being vain about one's knowledge, wisdom, or ability.

Our goal in this chapter is not to ask you to replicate certain communities of faith, such as St. Tim's, or even to mimic their programs. If you want to borrow or adapt something you read here, go for it! But even more important is the task of reflecting on the examples shared here and listening for a whisper of the Holy Spirit to lead you to try something new or to build on what you're already doing—to be willing to admit there are much more learning and growth God wants for you. This is about practicing the virtue of humility. The kind of personal and communal transformation we heard about at St. Tim's, the kind of spiritual depth and change that they have experienced, shines from the faces of the people we met there. Their storytelling was marked by modesty and quiet dignity. They truly believe that God is at work in their lives, in their priest, and in their parish community to change them for the better and for the sake of the world God loves. This is not merely a matter of change for the sake of change. This isn't just about catching the latest fad. This is not a capitulation to the false god called Novelty. This is a genuine conviction that as a learning community, and because they are learning and practicing the spiritual life, the people of St. Timothy's are better able to respond wisely and generously to the rapidly changing world around them. Their groups and projects are genuine, intentional efforts to be and build transformative, meaningful community in the Age of Loneliness. Multiple opportunities to learn and grow in group settings provide multiple entry points for newcomers as they try to meet other new people and find a way to belong. And continuous learning is also part of the ancient Christian understanding of sanctification: growing in grace, drawing closer to God, developing our gifts, and putting them to use as we serve our community together. Learning nourishes both our curiosity and our faith. It deepens our wisdom and reminds us that we have companions on the journey. It helps us become what we are meant to be. And the virtue of humility helps light the path toward that transformation.

It won't be a surprise that we (Russ and Rob) are big fans of learning. As ministers and professors, we've enjoyed lifetimes of formal education and the blessings it brings. We've loved it so much that we embraced the teaching life ourselves. Beyond formal and academic learning, we've treasured nonformal and nonrational learning through camping, outdoor living, sports, yoga, drama, dream interpretation, art, music, film, poetry, and relationships. You might fairly suspect that such a love of learning is ripe in us to project onto others, to assume that they are just like us. But we can honestly tell you that we discovered that a great many of the thriving Christian communities we met are also seriously and joyfully invested in learning and spiritual practice. They are embodying a profound and ancient Christian dynamic: they are discovering what it means to be disciples.

SIGNS OF GRACE AND WISDOM

Disciple is the English word for the Greek noun *mathētēs* as it's found in the Second Testament, referring to Jesus's closest followers. This word and its related verb form occur some 260 times in the Second Testament. *Mathētēs* could be more directly translated as "learner." The followers of Jesus were his learners, his students, his apprentices. Ever since then, the Christian movement has prized this spirit of learning. John Calvin wrote about having a "teachable heart" as one of the great virtues of a Christian. Scottish biblical scholar William Barclay once wrote, "All his [her, their] life, a Christian should be learning more and more about Jesus. The shut mind is the end of discipleship."[1] To be a disciple of Jesus and to practice humility is all about being open to where the Spirit might lead us or what God might show us through our encounters with anything, from the study of Scripture to a spontaneous conversation with someone waiting in line at the market. Noticing the movement of God in the world is an art that local communities of faith can become experts in. We can coach one another into this habit, this art. We can learn and practice specific things that strengthen the spiritual muscle. All the opportunities that local congregations and groups can offer people in order to learn, develop, discover, and grow are truly core to Christian identity. It would be wrong for any Christian to say, "I've got it all figured out" or for any congregation to say, "We've learned as much as we need to." Reluctance to learn is a kind of unfaithfulness and an expression of hubris—overweening pride, the opposite of humility. In contrast, eagerness to learn is a sign of grace and wisdom. Indeed, it is a sign of our vulnerability before a good and wonderful God, who continually has things to reveal to us. It is being open to God's ways of nurturing and shaping us as we become faithful followers of Jesus.

Another congregation we visited—Highview City Church—has been closely focused on spiritual growth and nurture since it was founded in the 1980s. They consider this to be key to why they are thriving today. When we met with the folks at Highview, it was clear that their approach also is characterized by humility. The focus on spiritual growth and nurture is more than saying "children's ministry matters" or "we should have a youth group." Instead, the congregation and its leaders (both paid ministers and lay volunteers) explicitly try to listen to how God is working in their lives and to focus on becoming more and more aligned with that. What a refreshing difference from so many of us who bump along from year to year, not giving much attention to our personal spiritual growth! That spiritual apathy is understandable if we have not built up a congregational culture that values this.

At Highview, small groups are the cornerstone of their approach. Of course, small group ministry is nothing new. You even could say that Jesus was the original small group ministry leader, calling twelve disciples together to live and learn as they traveled through life with him. The contemporary refocus on small groups started in the 1970s, inspired by the

Methodist "class meeting" system that John Wesley instituted in the 1700s. Wesley wanted his Methodist people to gather during the week to reflect on their walk with God, so he set aside times and places for them to meet, pray, and share their hearts. The class meetings, as he called them, were a central part of the success of early Methodism. Ordinary people were brought into a stronger, more loving, and wiser relationship as disciples of Jesus. Class meetings were a process of discovering God's way and becoming better aligned with it in ordinary life.

So back to Highview City Church. Here everyone is welcome, and this message is communicated over and over, both inside the church and through external advertising and social media. People who visit the church relate that they do experience a genuine sense of welcome when they come to Highview. Some even describe it as akin to the feeling of coming home. But the message doesn't stop at "we're glad you're here." There is a persistent, gentle, continuous message telegraphed out to the people of Highview: we are a community that follows Jesus, and we are constantly learning about his Way. As one of their ministers put it, "We exist to enable everyday, ordinary people to walk the way of Jesus." Everyone is part of that. It's not just a special class for newcomers (although they do have one of those), it's not just for Sunday school kids (although there is a Sunday school program every week), and it's not just for youth (although youth have many opportunities to connect and grow in their faith at Highview). Learning about Jesus and his Way is a whole-church project, so to speak, and it goes on year-round. If you don't have a Bible, Highview makes sure you get one for free. If you're not sure about how to read it, they provide straightforward brief daily reading "guides" that include a short passage of Scripture and a couple of brief thoughts or questions. If you're ready for the next step up, there is "a monthly 'fifteen minutes with God' daily devotional" that guides you into looking at Scripture in terms of your daily life and your walk with God. At each step, there is that persistent message that growing in Christ is important. Worshippers are told, with a dose of grace and humor, "Just because you walk through those doors, and this happens to be a church, doesn't mean you are growing in Christ." The leadership makes it clear it is important to learn and grow in one's faith. It actually matters.

SMALL GROUPS AND MORE

Again, small groups are the essential components of this total approach to congregational discipleship. It's not just personal or private spiritual practices—as important as those are. The Alpha program, first developed at Holy Trinity Brompton Church in London, England, is a main feature of the lineup of programs that Highview offers. Its focus on learning about the Bible and the basics of the Christian view of life has been transformative for them. Remarkably, as many as 50 percent of the participants in the Alpha series at Highview are not members of their church. They throw it open to anyone who wants to take part, so there is a lot of mixing with people of other faith traditions (and none). Quite often, a closely bonded cohort forms through the Alpha experience, and they choose to carry on as a small group post-Alpha. The leadership of the church encourages this: "Our best goal is to lead people into a small group. We are really focusing on small groups these days." But the ministers are openhearted and gentle about whether it happens or not. There is no pressure to continue in a small group.

Other small groups spring up or are designed and organized around life stages, like young parents or retired people. One group meets "on a Tuesday morning at six o'clock at a local café." (Obviously, these are people who can be awake and coherent at that hour!) Many groups meet in individuals' homes, and some meet at the church building. Quite commonly, groups will read a book together that inspires their Christian walk. Newcomers are invited into a new small group from time to time and are taken through a program called "The Way," which is meant to introduce the experience of being part of the church and is always focused on Scripture and prayer. It is something like Alpha but perhaps less intense. Youth programming and even Sunday school are modeled on small group–style ministry. Two young adult groups meet, and they are fully and only online.

What is the model of small group ministry at Highview? One minister describes it like this: They aim to bring together groups of eight to ten people to meet weekly. What happens in the meetings? "Ideally, we talk about three things in those groups. One would be to check in on your life: What's God doing in your life? How are things going? And then the second would be to study some kind of Scripture together. We are trying to simplify these days, and just coming back to some Scripture is a good place to be. And then prayer, for one another, with one another. Those three main things in each of the groups would be our overall goal."

It's a remarkably simple model. It's easy to set up, easy to plan, easy to lead, and—this is crucial—easy to replicate. Once a participant has taken part in a small group like this and has grown comfortable with it, that person can easily become a leader or facilitator of another small group. No special training or guidebook is needed. And it doesn't have to be the minister or a paid person who leads the group. At Highview, this has provided big dividends, because they are able to mentor and encourage many laypeople to lead many small groups, and the groups can spring up and take off without all being crammed into the minister's workweek.

Faith formation and spiritual development happen in other ways as well. The church board has chosen to take time in every meeting for prayer. This is not just a cursory thirty-second prayer at the beginning; it occurs throughout the meeting, as needed. As one of the ministers put it, "Here the mindset really is, 'Hey, at any point if we feel the need to pray, let's pray. Let's just stop the meeting and we'll pray.'" Board members feel like their spiritual yearnings are welcome and are being fed while they conduct the business of the church. The staff and worship planning teams also strive to nurture their faith even while they are doing the "work" of leading the church. This mindset is intentional and focused. As one of the ministers told us, "That's a phrase around here: *What God does in us is as important as what God does through us.*"

On Sunday mornings, in addition to the spiritual benefit of celebrating God in the hour of worship, people are encouraged to take home a key learning or a key practice and make it part of their daily life in the week ahead, such as a way to pray, a way to serve others, or a song refrain to sing. The dividing wall between Sunday morning and the rest of the week is specifically demolished. One of the ministers told us, "We put a 'going deep' question in the bulletin for every week so that people can take that home. It's on an insert page so that it's got the Scripture and often the words to a song." The physical take-home is a reminder of the spiritual practice but also a tangible gift from their church that helps them remember how important spiritual growth really is.

Highview is a congregation that works from the top to the bottom and from childhood to old age to encourage spiritual growth and nurture. Even before people darken the door of the church building, they know that this is a priority. It is repeated frequently in the worship services. It is reflected in the range of small group opportunities and the resources provided for a personal devotional life. It is practiced in the lay leadership and staff leadership teams. The net result is that Highview is a thriving, vibrant hub of the Holy Spirit. Other communities of faith and leaders (laypeople and ministers) turn to them for inspiration and coaching.

IT'S (NOT) SIMPLE: CHANGE OR DIE

Being a community of learning and spiritual practice has other benefits as well, including flexibility and adaptability—and avoiding extinction. The "known" and "usual" realities of a congregation's life are accepted but not treated like eternal and forever dynamics. Things change, and the world changes. A learning community is already predisposed to tackle the challenges of shifting circumstances. As James Russell Lowell wrote in his nineteenth-century poem,

> *New occasions teach new duties*
> *Time makes ancient good uncouth.*[2]

The pace of change in contemporary society is breathtaking, and it's hitting church participation especially hard. A recent study by the Pew Research Center tells it like it is:

> The Christian share of the U.S. population is declining, while the number of U.S. adults who do not identify with any organized religion is growing. . . . Moreover, these changes are taking place across the religious landscape, affecting all regions of the country and many demographic groups. While the drop in Christian affiliation is particularly pronounced among young adults, it is occurring among Americans of all ages. The same trends are seen among whites, Blacks and Latinos; among both college graduates and adults with only a high school education; and among women as well as men.[3]

A parallel set of data is not available for the Canadian context, but we suspect it would reveal similar trends.

This presents all Christian communities, and certainly those in the mainline, with an incredible challenge. Yet a congregation committed to learning is unafraid of "new occasions." This is a major asset in the hyper-connected digital age and indeed in the pandemic age in which we write this book. We can't sit still and hope the world will slow down to match our step. United Church of Canada minister Christine Jerrett recently wrote that the kind of communities of faith we are exploring in this book "have the capacity to respond and adapt quickly to emerging opportunities. Their leaders are less focused at maintaining stability and managing the system and more focused on cultivating an ecosystem where people are learning how to listen to God, to each other, and to their context, with humility and openness. The system encourages people to engage in experiments: starting new expressions of faith and surrendering or re-inventing older expressions of faith that are no longer working well."[4]

In nature, we know that organisms that fail to adapt to changing environments are doomed to die. Congregations are no different. This doesn't mean selling out to the culture. But it might mean abandoning the ways that lead to death and decline. Margaret Wheatley, the management consultant and systems analyst, suggests that the natural world shows us that life sustains itself "through shifts, crises, and catastrophes. All of this is possible and commonplace as long as the [living] system remains open, willing to learn and adapt. . . . However, if a living system closes itself off, there is no possibility for change and growth."[5]

Change is not only a game for younger people, however. Our elders are incredibly resourceful and wise in this work. We (Russ and Rob) were amazed by how many older folks exuded calm and patience through the early months of the COVID-19 crisis. They've already seen many troubles in life, from world wars to recessions to civil unrest to personal grief and more. They are resilient. The minister of South Valley Church, whom we will profile in chapter 5, recently spoke to a group of older women about their role in helping the church change:

I've pastored some congregations through some pretty big changes,
and every time the people who best coped with the change were the

old people, especially the seriously old people, the people who had seen unbelievable changes in their lifetime and because of that retained an attitude of fearlessness about change. This summer, a man in my church died at the age of one hundred. He was born on the kitchen table on the farm, rode to high school on a horse, went to war, and spent years in a POW camp. He spent the last part of his life bent over his stick and somewhat isolated by his loss of hearing. To stay connected, he kept up with the offspring and their offspring by looking at pictures of them and sending messages to them on an iPad. As you can imagine, someone who has lived through that kind of change is pretty fearless about change. It's a wonderful gift that we older folks can give to younger folks, our ability to cope with loss, our sense of proportion about coping with change. . . . To do that, it helps to be old.[6]

Sometimes we are called upon to practice a gracious relinquishing of what we have known. Even the precious and beloved aspects of our life together in congregations sometimes have to be released to an honorable death. We feel the pain of this deeply, especially when they are things that have nurtured, fed, and sustained us over the years. There is real grief in letting go. But a congregational culture that emphasizes learning and walking in the Holy Spirit's paths makes it easier for us to be faithful and calm in saying goodbye to old ways. Again, this is not about change for the sake of change. That kind of fetishization of change is an idol. Saying goodbye to old ways must always be in service to the greater good of God's purposes in us, in our communities of faith, and in our world. The natural world is full of examples of change and adaptation. It is intrinsic to evolution. The only other alternative is death.

This is worth saying again: when the environment changes, the organism (or organization) must change or die. The Christian church and local congregations are no different. We can watch the changes in society with disdain or bewilderment, but if all we do is watch, we will die on the sidelines. The Body of Christ will rot, not flourish. If we're lucky, our tombstones will just say, "There used to be a church here." We'll still be shaking our stubborn, ghostly fists at the world, blaming everyone but ourselves.[7]

THE GOOD SURPRISES
OF SPIRITUAL GROWTH

To its own surprise, Lakeside Church has recently embraced lifelong learning and spiritual growth. Their profile in the local community as a gathering place for public events and meetings, high school graduations, and large funerals made them a well-known fixture for many years, even to those who are not members. But the key to their status as a "thriving" church is their strong commitment to shaping people's faith and encouraging their walk with God. By their own admission, this internal culture of spiritual growth is a relatively new phenomenon, however. As an "establishment church," business models and a secular identity predominated in many aspects of their life together. Study groups were infrequent, and shared prayer was rare outside of Sunday morning worship. When a new ministry team arrived, this all began to shift. The new ministers encouraged them to think and talk about the "e-word"—evangelism. As a mainline and liberal congregation, the people of Lakeside found this to be a term and a concept that made them squirm. But persistent, patient conversation about the "e-word," laced with gentle good humor, started to make evangelism a more normal thing to talk about. As one layperson related the story,

> That came with the [new ministers]. It was not here before that. That was absolutely a gift that they brought to the church. We can talk about it; we can use the "e-word"! . . . That was scary for a lot of people. It happened in different ways and was subtle. They said, "Let's talk about it! How are we going to do this? Let's actually pray out loud and start our meetings with prayers and close with prayers." It took a long time to filter, but there are a lot more people more comfortable. When they left, that hasn't gone away. It wasn't about them. . . . That, to me, was a huge change at [our church].

Slowly but surely, the people of Lakeside Church started to realize that they themselves were the ones who needed to be evangelized. It wasn't about going "out there" and buttonholing people and waving the Bible at them. As a lay leader said, "Evangelism . . . has arrived [for Lakeside], and God is in it. . . . Now, people aren't afraid to pray with someone. I think because we had that invitation [from our ministers]. . . . So people are more comfortable with it, and I've actually seen it happen. With volunteers going out to visit or having coffee with someone and just saying, 'Can I pray with you?' It is happening."

This spilled over into their youth programming as well. It was always strong, but it was mostly about social events and games. Kids knew they'd have fun at that church. But a shift has been taking place: "I have to go back to . . . young people. My grandson . . . is part of the youth group, and he's very comfortable talking about his faith to his peers. . . . The youth leadership [started to say], 'We're actually going to talk about our faith, and we're going to learn to pray, and we're going to get down to the basics.' That had been something that was missing in the Christian education for quite a while."

Similarly, a retreat for women honed in on the spiritual growth potential for its participants and was no longer just a social event: "There was some prayer, there was . . . quiet time, listening time . . . taking on a caring role for another person, walking along, listening to their story, or listening to them. Not solving it, but listening and prayerfully keeping them."

Lakeside's commitment to spiritual growth among its members has given it a new and different profile in the community. This is still a growing edge for them, as their identity is starting to change. From being an establishment church, dominated by mostly secular forms, it is becoming a place where people go to find spiritual renewal. One interviewee told us, "Just this past Sunday, there was a new mom with her daughter, and she said, 'We're here because we heard there's something happening here.' I think it's a church where . . . something is actually happening, which I would describe as God's presence in a place. To me, God's presence is something that's profoundly contagious that people are drawn to."

Their deeper connection to a life of prayer and their growing Biblical literacy as a congregation has given them a new vision of what God is doing in and through them. When asked for a biblical image that describes their community of faith, one person said, "I'm going to go with Moses encountering God in the burning bush, because, how I make that connection is, Moses heard God's promise to the Israelites: 'I'm taking you to a land of milk and honey, to a land of fullness, a land of abundance,' and the sense that God's future is a hopeful, abundant future. That's something that's in the people in this church. A belief that we do have a hopeful, abundant future as part of God's mission in this place."

The humility of giving up one way of being church and learning a new way—becoming a community committed to spiritual growth—is a gift from God. Something is going on in this church that they didn't expect. Although one ministry team helped get the ball rolling, the momentum is still underway after they've departed. It is sinking more deeply into the DNA and ethos of the laypeople. Their spiritual hunger is being fed in a new way, and they welcome it eagerly.

A FRESH VISION

From St. Timothy's to Highview to Lakeside, we've found fresh visions of the good news that God is still at work! God is still motivating and empowering people (young and old) and faith communities to learn about, embody, and announce the justice and hope of the gospel. They are growing in faith, deepening their relationship with God, and trusting God's leading. They are praying and discovering the Bible and other spiritual practices in dynamic and life-changing ways. Broader and broader circles of engagement are drawing people into exploring and developing their faith. Creative, embodied, artistic, and kinesthetic forms of spirituality are emerging in new ways. Indigenous elders relate that in their communities, recovery of the sweat lodge, ancestral stories and teachings, powwows, dances, smudging, pipe ceremonies, and the use of traditional medicines are deepening and expanding the faith of the people. Those of us in the majority culture have much to learn from these ancient sources of wisdom.

The key question for the mainline church is not "How shall we die?" The key question is "How shall we join in what God is doing and live?" The best way to answer that question is to cultivate the virtue of humility and become a community of learning and spiritual growth.

QUESTIONS FOR DISCUSSION

1. What practices and habits of learning and spiritual development in your faith community do you think are working well? What do you like about them?

2. What spiritual practice or program would you like to try out to help your faith community and its people grow in the Spirit?

3. What do you think of the idea that a faith community humbly committed to learning and willing to change helps it to be more faithfully responsive to societal changes?

TWO CHALLENGES

1. Gather a small group along the lines of Highview Church's model. Include time to check in on how things are going for the group members, time with Scripture, and time to pray together. Meet for six weeks, and then take stock. Is there interest in continuing? Does something need tweaking in the model to better fit your context?

2. Contact another local congregation (or link with one online) and explore the possibility of sharing a spiritual growth program together. You don't have to do everything on your own!

OPENHEARTED LEADERSHIP
The Virtue of Love

A couple of years ago, a departing minister held her final service with her congregation and then stayed to receive hugs, handshakes, and well-wishes until every worshipper had left and she found herself alone. Then she walked to the front of the sanctuary, lay down on the floor, and carried out her own, private ritual of surrender. This was a surrender not to exhaustion or relief but rather to gratitude. She allowed herself to be held by an all-encompassing gratefulness for everything she had received, for everything she had witnessed, and for everything that she and her fellow leaders had accomplished over twenty years—which was considerable indeed.

This act of lying prone on the floor of a church may seem strange for a minister of a Protestant denomination known for cultural reserve, but it was pure Katya. She is nothing if not embodied. One feels it in her hugs and in the quality of her listening. She has that special gift of making the person with whom she is talking feel like the center of her world—and for that moment he is. One also experiences it in her leadership of worship, in the warmth that emanates from her. The only way she could have said goodbye to her beloved faith community was through an act of the body and the heart.

Katya's private rite was the final act of a truly successful pastoral relationship. Twenty years earlier, she had been greeted with some trepidation as the new (and first female) senior minister of University Street Church. As one parishioner later put it, "We were terrified that you were a raving feminist who would just preach *at* us—but you always *included us* in your preaching." He was putting his finger on one strand of her leadership DNA.

It was not Katya's way to do things *at* her parishioners. Her way was to do things *with* them, through the heart. As she put it, her pastoral relationship woke up a sleepy church: "They had fine bones, but they were asleep. I woke them up, and I did it by leading from the heart. University Street Church always had esteemed, white, male intellectuals for senior ministers. I took it another way, and I didn't even know I was doing it. I'm not sure I was curious enough intellectually, but I had a heart for it. The congregation loved me, and I returned that love. It wasn't a great prophetic turn; it was a turn through love." Indeed, her leadership always has been grounded in the virtue of love.

TURNING INWARD, TURNING OUTWARD

This "turn through love" is a powerful story. University Street Church (USC) was an old establishment church. It was founded about the same time as the large university a block away and by some of the same people. When Katya arrived, the connections between the church and the university were deep and strong but fading. Like most universities, it was casting off its links to Christianity. Still, the culture of USC resonated with the values fostered by those original connections: intellectual thirst, progressive theology, personal reserve, and caution when it came to considering change. As its traditional membership catchment of intellectuals migrated away from organized religion, USC was shrinking. A new form of community engagement was needed, and for this, a new model of church had to come about.

The model that emerged required, paradoxically, both a turning inward and a turning outward. To paraphrase Katya, the vision was that USC would be like a medieval cathedral for this city. It would be the spiritual beat of that place. They wanted to be where the heartbeat of the community was; accomplishing this required throwing open the church doors to the city at large, inviting in non-Christians, and hosting non-faith-based events. It also required going into the city to build relationships with many diverse groups. These actions were part of the plan to turn outward. But if USC was to host the heartbeat of the city, it had to know its *own* heartbeat better. Put another way, Katya and her collaborators had to attend to two relationship webs: the relationship web of the city and the relationship web within USC. Love for the city and love for the people of the congregation went hand in hand.

According to the model, if USC is to engage the relationship web of the city through acts of friendship, solidarity in action, and hospitality, those same acts need to be performed between groups and individuals within USC. At first, it was often Katya modeling them with her leadership partners. Shared spiritual practices became a key medium. Katya and a lay leader offered opportunities for spiritual development and personal growth throughout the church year. They included a mindfulness group, annual Advent retreats, silent Lenten retreats, yearly women's retreats, weekend family retreats, and a program called Nine to Dine, which gathered nine people for nine dinners.

One group was made up of women on the cusp of retirement. When these women were identified, they were invited to meet monthly and participate in a yearly retreat. Often this led to forms of lay leadership, including a parish nurse position. The parish nurse was supported to receive training in the area of mental health, and now she has an ongoing ministry to provide similar training for the congregation. This is one of many examples in which a layperson became a member of the ministry staff without receiving payment. They become covenanted members of the team and are expected to perform on a par with salaried ministers. And they do, infusing the leadership circle with diversity and vitality. Leadership on all levels is encouraged and embraced in a culture of support and love.

This careful practice of building strong relationships and going deep together within the USC congregation is replicated in the ways USC's leaders weave a web of relationships in the larger community. Early in Katya's tenure, USC decided to sell off a piece of property adjacent to the church. Given its location, this property would bring in several million dollars if sold to high-end developers. Instead, it was sold for a fifth of its potential value to a group that turned it into low-income housing. The money from the sale was used to renovate a part of the main church complex to host a school. USC then went through a long process of dialoguing with potential tenants to see which of them best fit its values. Again, maximizing income was not at the top of the priority list.

When it comes to hosting events for the larger community, the same principles are applied. One of its first new programs was organized around spiritual practice co-led by Christian and Buddhist teachers. After 9/11, joint events were organized with Muslims, and an imam was invited to preach on Sunday morning. USC sponsors a group whose goal is to create friendship with a Middle Eastern country that is often associated with terrorism in the media. It organized exchange trips. Lecture series and cultural events with low prices of admission are hosted for the city with well-known speakers and performers. Relationships are fostered with the Roman Catholic community center at the university, a synagogue, and a number of Protestant congregations. These relationships place USC at the center of a kind of congregation of congregations, which then jointly organize social actions on issues of race, same-sex marriage, playground space for children, and poverty.

Eventually, USC's medieval cathedral model was very much realized, and to an impressive extent, it *has* come to host the heartbeat of the city. Taking a look at USC's recent history as though from several hundred feet above with an eagle's eye view, this is what one sees: Katya and a few coleaders at the center, hosting the heartbeat of USC and holding the congregation's relationship web in their affection and care. Letting one's focus widen, one then sees USC hosting with affection and care a much larger relationship web that extends throughout the city. This new model for the church contains many elements we want to hold up as we consider leadership:

- truly vital symbiosis—a synergy—between ordained/designated ministers and lay leaders

- leaders who are both strong and vulnerable

- leaders who are both empathic and differentiated

- continuous, deep listening

- inseparability of the two vocations of spiritual practice and justice seeking

- opening of the soul that involves simultaneously turning inward and turning outward

- belief on the part of leaders that the internal and external webs of relationship are inseparable and must be held with affection and care

- deep trust in the presence of the Divine, which allows a faith community to choose spiritual capital over financial capital when such a choice is necessary

- embeddedness in the Community of Heaven, which draws all relationships and all practices down into the mycelia, the Ground of Being[1]

Undergirding all these elements—embracing them and providing the key to USC's renewal—is one essential trait: an openness of heart. Multiple forms of openness can be seen in the above list: openness to shared leadership; the uncomfortable openness that comes with vulnerability; internal openness to one's depths and external openness to others (including those very different from themselves); the, sometimes scary, openness to the Divine, who might upend our plans and challenge our closely held truths at any turn. This openness of heart doesn't just mean being compassionate and having warm feelings, even if they are important elements; it also means a kind of gentle strength, and sometimes that strength involves differentiation, the telling of difficult truths, and the capacity to hold (sometimes passionate) differences of opinion without premature resolution. Like love, courage is also associated with the heart.

In chapter 1 of this book, we wrote of a pervasive death drive in the mainline church and identified two key causes: a surrender to the scientific materialist worldview of our culture and denial and confusion over the church's complicity in colonialism. When we review what we have learned about USC, we are struck by how brightly it stands as a counterexample and attribute this to its openhearted leadership marked by gentle strength.

Given USC's long and deep connection to the university, it is no easy feat to resist the worldview of scientific materialism. Consistent spiritual practices of multiple kinds appear to be essential to that resistance. So do ongoing interfaith relationships. These same relationships, and those with social enterprise groups, are also critical in responding to the legacy of colonialism. USC is made up mostly of privileged white people. Its consistent encounter with racialized persons and with those struggling with poverty, Islamophobia, the legacy of the Shoah (or Holocaust), and heterosexism has shrunk its blind spots. These outward-reaching initiatives force the congregation to examine how systemic racism has built the structures of wealth and power upon which their privilege rests. By no means have the blind spots fully disappeared, but the ways USC allocates its resources and invests in diverse relationships show real progress in the long, long process of confronting the colonial project.

HOT-WIRED AND EVANGELICAL—IN THE MAINLINE?

At this point, we want to introduce you to another leader and to compare his leadership with Katya's. Dave is a minister at Westside Church, a thriving congregation in an urban/suburban community in central Canada. In many ways, he is a perfect contrast to Katya. Where she is post-Christian cool, he is hot-wired and sounds evangelical. Her presence is smooth and fluid and seems to cast a gentle light. His presence is intense, his words come in staccato bursts, and he seems to fire out quanta of energy that bounce around the room in all directions. Katya's way of seeing the world has been shaped by interfaith engagement, ecological exploration, and the play of improvisational drama. Dave's has been molded by the experiences of intense Bible study and charismatic prayer. She resonates most with the Creator, the First Person of the Trinity. He is bursting with love for the Second Person, Jesus Christ.

Despite all these differences, Dave's and Katya's ministries have taken them to surprisingly similar places: a gospel of inclusion, full embrace of sexual minorities and people of other faiths without the impetus to convert, focused action in solidarity with the poor and the marginalized, effective ministries of invitation, and deep engagement with the larger community. Westside Church may not function as the "heartbeat of the city" in exactly the same way as USC does, but Dave's city elected him Citizen of the Year a couple of years ago.

So is there a common core characteristic these two leaders share that has engendered vitality in both of them? There is. It is a *continual opening to a reality that is larger and deeper than themselves*: God's love. The experience of surrender is shaped by our personalities, each of us entering into it and emerging from it with our own distinct qualities. Katya's surrender is to the Divine, personal and impersonal, immanent and transcendent—sometimes available as presence, sometimes available as absence, mysterious and paradoxical. Dave's surrender comes across as less relaxed and less marked by paradox. Here is how he answered some of our questions. When asked why he came to serve this church, he said, "It was a church that had a vital faith. Clarity around Christ. Very Spirit led." When he was asked whom that church was currently attracting, he remarked,

> We would name the presence of God that is here, and we're just grateful for that. We keep saying, let's not take that for granted.... I would say that we have reached certain groups of people because of some of the outreach work we've done. One example is a neighborhood in a nearby municipality we've been working in. There has been lots of publicity around it because there have been some tragedies. We name it as an area that just needs some TLC [tender loving care] and that God loves it and God is already there, and we've gone in to love this neighborhood with God. As a result of that, we have people from that community who are now part of our church.

When we asked how Westside Church gave "tender loving care" to the people of that nearby community, Dave gave several specific examples but prefaced them with this: "Sure, well, it started by just being there. Going there. We read a Scripture, John 1:14, and *The Message* translation said, 'The Word became flesh . . . and moved into the neighborhood.' Well, that is the gospel. God took on human flesh, and we're invited to do the same. We need to move into these neighborhoods, and that's just the way God is working in our church's life."

Westside has adopted the practice of following a theme in worship over several weeks to explore its various aspects and implications for contemporary life and faith. When asked about successes and failures of that approach, Dave said, "So our learning over the years is the more we struggle with a series, the more God intends to bless it. Because there's a reason that we're struggling. It's a deep issue."

Upon hearing language like this, some liberal Christians might be tempted to write Dave off as an "evangelical" or a "conservative" and not one of them. But Dave is rigorously nonjudgmental, deeply committed to justice work, and strongly supportive of LGBTQ+ liberation. Many in the mainline would be less threatened by Katya's kind of surrender to the

Divine: it is less categorical, less certain, seemingly less disposed to inspire aggression in mission. But Dave and Westside Church have found a way to throw themselves into the fire of Christ whenever they encounter trouble, gritty realities, or doubt. They trust transformation and are refined without taking on the armor of aggressive Christianity. They engage the larger culture without a hint of motivation to reestablish the colonial project of Christendom. Talking to lay members of Westside, it became clear to us that Dave's constant "yes" to the presence of God is infectious. In a virtuous circle, their commitment to the living reality of God attracted Dave to them, and he lives it with them as they grow.

ENCOUNTERING GOD OR JUST THINKING ABOUT GOD?

We want to dwell on this point for a while because we think there is a lesson here that is essential for the mainline church. Many of us who have known this church for decades are concerned about something we perceive, something paradoxical. While our worldview may have become more inclusive, we have often become less friendly, less generous, and more fearful. There has been a closing of the heart. As we argued in the opening chapter, there are many reasons for this. Here we want to highlight one more.

In the liberal church, there has been a drift from understanding God as someone we *encounter* to someone we *think about*. We spend less time listening for God's whispers and more time trying to "define" God so that we can have a concept of the Divine that is acceptable to the larger culture. We want our understanding of God to be palatable to minds (including our own) that have been shaped in an ethos of scientific materialism. But all this conceptualizing has turned us away from *perceiving* God, away from being open to seeing the Divine animating the world around us, and away from allowing the Spirit to massage open our hearts.

Philosopher and media theorist Marshall McLuhan saw this shift decades ago, and reversing it was a key aspect of his conversion to Roman Catholicism. McLuhan's son, Eric, writes about this in the introduction to his father's book *The Medium and the Light: Reflections on Religion*: "This distinction between concept and percept, ideas and sheer awareness, became crucial to revealing much in media study and in meditating upon the church and related matters. McLuhan wrote to Jim Taylor, then editor of the *United Church Observer*, that he did 'not think of God as a concept, but as an immediate and ever-present fact—an occasion for continuous dialogue.'"[2] In the elder McLuhan's own words, this is how his conversion happened:

> I had no religious belief at the time I began to study Catholicism. . . . I didn't believe anything. I did set to find out, and literally, to research the matter, and I discovered fairly soon that a thing has to be tested on its own terms. You can't test anything in science or in any part of the world except on its own terms. The church has a very basic requirement or set of terms, namely that you get down on your knees and ask for the truth. . . . I prayed to God the Father for two or three years, simply saying, "Show me." I didn't want proof of anything. I didn't know what I was going to be shown because I didn't believe in anything.
>
> I was shown very suddenly. It didn't happen in the expected way. It came instantly as immediate evidence, and without any question of its being a divine intervention. There was no trauma or personal need. I never had any need for religion, any personal or emotional crisis. I simply wanted to know what was true and I was told. . . . Wham! I became a Catholic the next day.[3]

This "yes" to God, not as a concept that can be debated but as an *agent* in our lives with whom we can dialogue daily, is the most important "yes" that church leaders can embrace today. This embrace is absolutely countercultural—and we are talking about the culture of the mainline church as much as the culture of our society. When God is a mere concept, then church renewal is only something we can *think about*. It becomes completely dependent on human skill and human capacity to interpret the culture around us, which is seemingly changing by the nanosecond. More helpful would be to replicate McLuhan's two or three years on his knees saying, "Show me." In our experience, it rarely takes a faith community engaged in spiritual practice this long to be shown glimpses of a future that vibrates with Divine energy. Perhaps this is because, unlike McLuhan, churches of today do tend to find themselves in an emotional crisis when they fall to their knees.

THE COMMUNITY OF HEAVEN

What kind of theological work will help Christian leaders with all this—those of us who are trying to serve communities embedded in both an intellectual world of scientific materialism and a cultural world that smells the stench of colonialism wafting from the church? The heart of this theological work is a reality to which Jesus pointed again and again in his teaching: the Community of Heaven. In English translations of the Second Testament, traditionally it has been rendered as the "Kingdom of Heaven" (*basileia tōn ouranōn*) or the "Kingdom of God" (*basileia tou theou*). Much of Jesus's teaching was oriented to helping his listeners recognize this realm, which was present to their lives. He taught that the "kingdom" was "within you," or "among you" (Luke 17:21), a living dynamic with the potential to reshape individuals, families, communities, and whole societies in harmony with God's love. Many of his parables were taught to help his listeners adjust their consciousness into resonance with this realm and to help them live in God's way.

The Greek term *basileia* is the Second Testament word used to refer to this realm (although Jesus may have spoken in Aramaic). While *basileia* is usually translated into English as "kingdom," it also can be translated as "empire," which is helpful for our discussion here. *Empire* evokes the notion that Jesus was speaking of God's realm as powerful and vast as the Roman Empire, and even more so, but with antithetical values. Rome was imposing its theology of emperor worship, its economics of scarcity and extraction, and its politics of conquest on Palestine. Jesus proclaimed an empire marked by a theology of love, an economics of abundance, and a politics of "the last will be first, and the first will be last" (Matt 20:16).

Because of its patriarchal resonance, many scholars and preachers have rejected the term *kingdom of heaven* and have chosen instead *reign*, *realm*, *commonwealth*, or *kindom of heaven*. This latter term picks up the idea that all in God's realm are "kin": family in the household of the Divine. We choose to use the term "Community of Heaven." Like *kindom*, it also implies the collective good, mutuality, interdependence, and regard for others' well-being.

The Community of Heaven is alive and well and living "within us and among us." It may be that the Community of Heaven's existence in human consciousness is akin to a kind of quantum potentiality. In the quantum realm, things can be understood to "exist" only as probabilities or potentialities. An agent, such as a human being, can actualize a potentiality, making it a reality in our world of experience. So the Community of Heaven can be continually emerging, becoming real, in our midst. The Community of Heaven resonates with a future much more in tune with God's love and God's values and holds that future before us, inviting us to step into it.

In chapter 1, we claimed that the key move for a faith community seeking revitalization was a move *down* into depth, into the Ground of Being (mycelia), which is God. Another way to articulate this is to say that the key move is into the Community of Heaven, which emerges from the Ground of Being and which holds before us an emerging future. That future is already alive—at least in potentiality—and it invites us into a way of living in resonance and alignment with God's love. This move *down* at its most powerful is an entry into the *heart of God*. Here any impetus to power is changed to an impetus to love, even if that love requires self-sacrifice. Here we find the opposite of the "might is right" values of the Roman Empire and of any imperial project. Here we know that "love is right," even if it compels us to live in a way that seems foolish to the larger culture.

Just as this is the key move for a faith community, it is the key move of its leaders. Leaders who help a faith community come alive in a way that fills it with vitality and makes it useful to the larger world are leaders who immerse themselves in the Community of Heaven. Different leaders have different ways of doing this: some do it with prayer, some with deep listening to others, some in study of the Bible, some in action for justice, some in communion with nature, some in the work of reconciliation. Each of these things can become a form of prayer. Whatever form the immersion takes, it becomes tinged with a hint of holiness. It becomes saturated with love. When we take the time to listen to our deep selves, we know intuitively which practices open this door for us, which practices open our hearts. Katya knew this intuitively when she lay down in the sacred space of the USC sanctuary and surrendered.

It can be difficult for Christian leaders to shape their lives to do this regularly. It can be more than difficult to allow one's heart, and therefore one's actions, to be shaped in this way. A tragic paradox in mainline denominations is that a minister's work life is usually designed to preclude such practices. There is so much *busyness* in the business of church. There are so many damn meetings. There is so much anxiety. There is so much fear of failure, so much pressure to produce quantifiable results. And there is such forgetfulness when it comes to our tradition's wisdom for the care of the soul. When a minister does find her way into the slipstream of the Community of Heaven and comes to her church governing council with the advice that more attention needs to be given to matters of the Spirit and less to matters of the bottom line, she is very often met with blank stares—or outright resistance.

So what's a leader to do? The answer is straightforward, but it takes guts and a willingness to look like a fool in the eyes of the world and perhaps in the eyes of the congregation. He needs a little time every day, and bigger chunks of time every season and every year, to enter his spiritual practice and descend. He needs to find his own web of trusted friends who honor his way of going deep and will remind him when busyness or resistance is pulling him out of depth. As the leader of a workshop that Russ attended once put it, "You need to find your song and keep singing your song, *and* you need to form a choir of trusted friends who learn your song and keep singing it back to you, even when you have forgotten the words."

INSIGHT FROM OTTO SCHARMER

Otto Scharmer and his collaborators offer in their work something that looks very much like a description of the Community of Heaven. They write of something they call the "emerging future," which is described using secular language (although Scharmer does admit to being influenced by a number of theological and spiritual sources). A good starting point is an assertion by Scharmer and Katrin Kaeufer in their introduction to *Leading from the Emerging Future*: "The quality of results produced by any system depends on the quality of awareness from which people in the system operate. The formula for a successful change process is not 'form follows function' but 'form follows consciousness.' The structure of awareness and attention determines the pathway along which a situation unfolds."[4]

Similarly, Scharmer claims that "successful leadership depends on the quality of attention and intention that the leader brings to any situation. Two leaders in the same circumstances doing the same thing can bring about completely different outcomes, depending on the inner place from which each operates."[5]

Scharmer and his colleagues have set for themselves a very ambitious agenda: to respond to the full range of crises besetting our planet—ecological, social, psychological, and spiritual—which they see as inseparably connected. Their impact is beginning to meet the scale of their ambition. They have a vast readership, and many thousands of people are engaging with their learning networks.

Scharmer's approach argues that the various crises assailing our world are really one crisis that arises from three divides:

- the ecological divide: separation from nature

- the social divide: separation from others

- the spiritual divide: separation from self

They argue that humanity is making poor progress in responding to these divides and their symptomatic crises because leaders in all spheres operate from an acute blind spot. Leaders are conscious of huge volumes of data about the world's problems, but they are blind to the inner place from which they operate. Operating out of this blind spot, leaders continually engage in what Scharmer calls "downloading": repeating the same old forms of action, perhaps dressed in new clothes, over and over again, with the same results. This isn't far from the story of the mainline church over the last half century!

The first liberation from this stalemate, according to Scharmer and his coauthors, occurs when addressing the spiritual divide. That is where we must begin. This happens when leaders go through a multistep, U-shaped process of *descent* and *reascent*. At the bottom of the U comes awareness of two things: the place from which we operate and the presence of an emerging future that can speak to us. The reascent takes the form of co-creation with others. Scharmer's work resonates very much with what we have learned in our research. Using our language, we would describe the bottom of the U as the open heart. Both leaders and communities who find their way to the open heart become aware of the center from which they operate and aware of the future being offered by God. *Theory U* describes the five movements of the process of descent and reascent:

- *Co-initiating: Listen to what life calls you to do,* connect with people and contexts related to that call, and convene constellations of core players that co-inspire common intention.

- *Co-sensing:* Go to the places of most potential; observe, observe, observe; listen with your mind and heart wide open.

- *Co-presencing:* Go to the place of individual and collective stillness, open up to the deeper source of knowing, and *connect to the future that wants to emerge through you.*

- *Co-creating:* Build landing strips of the future by prototyping living microcosms in order to *explore the future by doing.*

- *Co-evolving:* Co-develop a larger innovation ecosystem and hold the space that connects people across boundaries through *seeing and acting from the whole.*[6]

It is striking how this progression describes exactly the process followed by Katya, her coleaders, and USC as a whole as it revitalized itself and embedded itself in a larger web of relationships, to which it also contributed great vitality. And this is true not only of USC but also of many, perhaps even most, of the faith communities we studied in the Thriving Christian Communities Project. Katya's private ritual on the floor of the USC sanctuary was an example of what Scharmer says is essential for getting to the bottom of the U and closing the spiritual divide: letting go. Here's an explanation in his words: "At the bottom of the U lies an inner gate that requires us to drop everything that isn't essential. This process of letting-go (of our old ego and self) and letting-come (our highest future possibility: our Self) establishes a subtle connection to a deeper source of knowing. The essence of presencing is that these two selves—our current self and our best future Self—meet at the bottom of the U and begin to listen and resonate with each other. Once a group crosses this threshold, nothing remains the same."[7]

The work of Scharmer and his partners is inspiring for three reasons. First, it describes so well how revitalization takes place within faith communities. Second, it gives Christian communities a model and a language for engaging the larger community (including interfaith and non-faith-based partners) in renewal processes without imposing Christian language upon these processes. Third, and perhaps most importantly, it offers a way of seeing church revitalization as deeply embedded in the work of responding to the world's three great divides (ecological, social, and spiritual) and all the crises that arise from them.

On the descent side of Scharmer's U-shaped process, and in no small measure on the ascent side as well, the key activity is *listening*. The core organ for this kind of listening is not the ear but the heart. Scharmer's books devote considerable space to this skill. This again resonates with what we have learned in our research and work lives as ministers and educators. Russ's experiences with truth and reconciliation processes in South Africa and Canada and with adaptive conversations in congregations[8] have impressed upon him the healing and transformational power of listening. When we drop into the deepest levels of listening, our hearts are held within the Divine heart, and thinking is replaced by loving as the strongest mode of understanding. When we interviewed the leaders of thriving faith communities, we kept finding people with this capacity. They were warm people. When we showed up, they trusted us and were curious about us and our work.

LISTENING, LISTENING, AND THEN LISTENING MORE

This reference to the heart is important. Oftentimes listening is simply thought of as paying attention to the *cognitive content* of what someone is saying to you, but it is so much more. Watching effective leaders in group interviews or focus groups, we witnessed the same thing we had seen in other transformative conversations like talking circles with Indigenous peoples or hearings in the respective South African and Canadian Truth and Reconciliation Commissions. Powerful listening has its own kind of descent through several stages:

- *Surface listening*, which is most common in everyday interactions, involves paying attention to the cognitive content of what someone else is saying with a certain percentage of one's mind while the rest of one's mind is attending to other things, such as what you are going to say when it's your turn to talk.

- *Second-level listening* occurs with the exercise of directed aware-ness. One grants almost 100 percent of one's attention to the speaker but is still mostly attending to cognitive content.

- *Empathic listening* expands the awareness to include attention to the speaker's feelings. Sometimes one actually starts to feel what the speaker is feeling. This can produce body sensations or a kind of visceral knowing.

- *Expansive listening* happens when the whole group of people in the conversation drops into a place of empathic listening and become aware of the feelings of the entire group, not just the one speaking at any given moment.

- *Transformative listening* has a touch of the holy. It is rare but is seen especially in a setting like a multiday talking circle when a group develops broad trust and shares deeply. When this occurs, wisdom beyond that possessed by individual members of the group enters the circle, as if coming up through the ground. The Holy Spirit becomes a participant both in listening and in speaking.

As an exercise for church leaders, we invite you to become (or continue to be) self-aware of the quality of your listening during a conversation or two each day. Exercise this kind of mindfulness. You'll notice yourself dropping through the stages in some conversations and receive some cues as to how to improve your skill. You also will notice the quality of your listening transforming conversations—even church meetings! Your listening will open up glimpses of light, hope, and the emerging future. You also might notice yourself developing greater affection for the people in your faith community, which will open up new possibilities.

An effective way to open the windows of a faith community to Christ's love is to train groups of lay folk in the stages of listening. They can then be invited to extend the ministry of listening throughout the many gatherings of a faith community: in the kitchen, at coffee hour, during meetings, in fellowship groups and Bible studies, and so on. When a critical mass of congregants starts to exercise this kind of care, a faith community transforms.

But what about listening to people who are operating from a place that feels like the opposite of love? How does a leader listen to the voice of anger, complaint, or resistance? How do we listen to those individuals (almost every church has them) who seem to believe that their core mission in life is to be oppositional and to attack leadership? Among the leaders we met and learned from, there was often an ability to listen attentively to discontented voices without allowing the voice of complaint to hold the community captive or to dominate meetings such that important decisions could not be faithfully taken.

The three issues we've just noted—the ministry of listening, ministry by lay leaders, and dealing with conflict—are all present in the story of Wesley St. David's (WSD) Church, the product of an amalgamation in a rapidly changing suburb of a large city. Like all amalgamations, the formation of WSD had its share of conflict. Responding to this and to the challenges that come with integrating two faith communities that have their own history, ethos, and internal narrative (different "angels," as Walter Wink might put it), WSD's leadership were keenly focused on intentionally shifting the culture through adaptive conversation. It helped that their minister, Deborah, already had been studying the work of Ron Heifetz, a pioneer in this area. It also helped that the newly formed congregation had a number of capable laypeople with relevant experience from their work lives. Deborah offers this reflection:

We had some smart people who had done this in other iterations in their lives. They knew the steps to follow. Shelly emerged as a brilliant process person. She knew how to do it intuitively, with a real gift for discerning a process. There were some technical things to it, too, but it was softer, more organic. It was a lot of listening. Listening to God, listening to the Spirit, and hearts were opened, hearts were opened! . . . I think it was a real sense of—it wasn't being driven—we're doing what we've been called to do and what we're led to do. It wasn't a forced mandate. . . . It was "What's the call?" And if there's a call, then we'd discern that call. Once we discerned a call, then our commitment was "We're going to make this work." After that, the people were on fire. After the visioning exercise, I was like, "OK, stand back, and watch it happen!"

This embrace of strong lay leadership and a synergy between ordained and lay leadership became a key trait of the emerging angel of Wesley St. David's Church. The training and identification of lay leaders happen through repeated faith formation processes. (We saw this in Highview City Church, too, back in chapter 3.) When newcomers join the church, they are expected to engage in a program that introduces them to Christian theology, the marks of discipleship, and the life of WSD. Deborah and her lay coleader of sixteen years lead this program. The next level of training offers foundations for lay leadership with explorations of spiritual practices, the enneagram, family systems, and so on.

All of this makes for a dynamic community with excellent leadership, affection, and toughness (when needed). Shortly before our visit, Deborah had to navigate some conflict that involved unhelpful behavior on the part of a small number of people. Here is how she talked about it:

> So back to the confrontation that was erupting in my office this past Sunday. Yes, I can be tough when I need to. Which is not about "get out of my office because I have to lead worship right now," but it's about the follow-up that happened after that. Which was around "You know what? If you're all going to be here in this congregation together, we're going to have a little mediated conversation, we're going to come up with a written agreement around behavior, and everyone is going to sign it. And that's how you're going to be here." If you can't do that, then that's your decision. That's what we do here in the Christian church. We talk to each other face-to-face about what's going on and what our problems are and what we perceive and what we're assuming about each other. We listen to each other. If you can't do that, then I guess you're not going to be here.

Deborah's intervention didn't come only from a place of ministerial power and authority but also from giving voice to community norms hard-won through adaptive conversation and shared leadership. It is a church with a healthy community and a healthy ecosystem.

So often churches fracture, weaken, or fail to make wise decisions at places like annual meetings or church councils because the groundwork of adaptive conversations and training lay leaders hasn't been laid.

Congregations like WSD stay healthy and vital even through rough patches or challenging times because of the work done over many years before. Reviewing our transcripts of the interviews at WSD, it was striking to hear Deborah and others speak frankly both about being tough and uncompromising on things like behavioral covenants *and* about listening to the Spirit and living with open hearts. In these times of anxiety in our congregations and parishes, it is not easy for leaders to maintain hearts big enough to be both soft and strong, but that is exactly what their faith communities need from them.

The stories of Katya, Dave, and Deborah, and their relationships to their faith communities (and to the larger world), are all marked by love, but one sees in them how diverse the qualities of love can be. Physicists teach us that the basic forces of the universe that govern all interactions—gravity, electromagnetism, the weak force, and the strong force—are related but diverse. Similarly, our research has taught us that the fundamental force in the world of human relations—God's love—is diverse in its expressions. Christian theology has discussed such expressions as *eros*, love in deep bonds of attraction; *philia*, love in friendship or sibling relations; and *agape*, unconditional love that often leads to sacrifice. How did Katya, Dave, Deborah, and the other dynamic leaders we studied find their own ways to embody divine love? How did they find ways appropriate to the contours of their churches and the larger community? Over and over, we saw that these were leaders willing to descend into the Ground of Being, the field of Divine Love, letting go of their certainties and trusting that the reascending would be marked with new wisdom, insight, and energy. This willingness to descend provided the "openness" part of being "openhearted," keeping the future rife with possibility. Their reascending was marked with *courage*. Courage is essential because rising up from an encounter with the Ground of Being almost always brings a leader or a faith community into some form of confrontation with the values and the assumed "wisdom" that characterize society, culture, and the institutional church. It is to the virtue of courage that we now turn.

QUESTIONS FOR DISCUSSION

1. Discuss the idea that the Community of Heaven is present in our lives all the time. Do you feel this in your own spiritual life? How is it present in your faith community?

2. Among the elements of leadership named in this chapter, discuss the ways these are present, or not present, in your faith community:

   - truly vital symbiosis—a synergy—between ordained/designated ministers and lay leaders

   - leaders who are both strong and vulnerable

   - leaders who are both empathic and differentiated

   - continuous, deep listening

   - inseparability of the two vocations of spiritual practice and justice seeking

   - opening of the soul that involves simultaneously turning inward and turning outward

   - belief on the part of leaders that the internal and external webs of relationship are inseparable and must be held with affection and care

   - deep trust in the presence of the Divine, which allows a faith community to choose spiritual capital over financial capital when such a choice is necessary

   - embeddedness in the Community of Heaven, which draws all relationships and all practices down into the mycelia, the heart of God

3. What are the ways that leaders of your faith community get to "go deep" together? Do you need to introduce more ways, and if so, how and where would you suggest starting?

TWO CHALLENGES

1. Design and lead a retreat for leaders of your faith community that focuses on leadership development through spiritual growth.

2. Try to live with an awareness of your experience of God and not just having a concept of God. The disciplines of mindfulness or meditation can be helpful in this.

5

WILLINGNESS TO RISK
The Virtue of Courage

Aversion to risk might be the key to building a conservative stock portfolio, but it's the death knell for local communities of faith. Willingness to risk is essential for thriving and vitality. It's the secret sauce of churches that are breaking out of the paradigm of decline and punching above their weight in terms of impact on the world around them. We're not talking about foolishness or foolhardiness. We're talking about risk as the readiness to say "yes!" to the call of God to break out of the norm and to become something new. If your congregation is dying, what have you got to lose? You might die anyway, but you'll go out with a spectacular bright flash of light. You'll be the pine cone that bursts open and scatters seeds to repopulate the forest. You already have read about how this has happened in some of the churches we visited, but there is so much more to learn!

THE STORY OF SOUTH VALLEY CHURCH

One congregation we met, South Valley, is so deeply convinced about the grace of God and so unconcerned with survival that they opt for the risk of faithfulness every chance they get. Traveling along the rural road that passes their building, you would see steam gently rising from the cornfields on a hot summer's day. The humidity would slow you down and make you look for some lemonade poured over a tall glass of ice. Driving by the church, you wouldn't see anything exceptional. It's a century-old white-gray stone structure that looks a bit worn out. The yard is full of overgrown trees and shrubs. Inside, the worship space is partially renovated but needs some attention. No one is in a hurry to finish it up. They have bigger priorities, like the needs of their neighbors. Their hearts (in French, "heart" is *coeur*—the root word for courage) are filled with imaginative responses to practical needs. They know by hard, joyful experience that it is costly to reach out. But they remain committed to it.

South Valley's need for an expanded worship space (seen in their still-unfinished renovations) has been on the radar for many years. Additional worship services were tried in a spirit of experimentation. Various configurations in terms of timing and style of service were developed over the years, but they kept returning to the desire for a larger sanctuary. Eventually, the decision was made to reconfigure the property, and it was a costly venture. As they put it, "there were growing pains and big decisions to make." But South Valley remained committed to their local mission work as well, staying connected to their neighbors and helping meet their needs even as South Valley spent money on the building. More remarkably, South Valley was doing this for the second time in living memory. That is, the building expansion was their second semisuccessful attempt to make such a project happen. The big difference is that the first time, they heard about a need for schools in a less-privileged country and decided to give to that, sacrificially, instead. Here is the story as one congregant shared it with us:

> Well, we had heard about a center in [a country] where they take in orphans, kids who have been orphaned by AIDS. AIDS is a huge problem in [that country]. As a congregation, we made a decision not to spend money on the expansion, so we had some money to share. We committed $200,000 to build two schools for this orphanage. . . . They were using what should have been dorm space for classrooms, and so we made a commitment to raise the money for them to go to preschool and a primary school so that they could move that out of the dorms and then take on some additional kids. In the first year, we sent three teams of people over to help do a variety of things, everything from tiling the floors to people who painted and made curtains and helped out in ways that we could help. . . . I think that it was an ambitious undertaking financially, because although there was some money that we kind of had set aside, there was a lot more that had to be raised [for the orphanage], and people responded very positively to that.

Another person from South Valley replied to that story sharing with the following:

> I think the congregation is brave to be involved with all these things because we could very easily say, "Oh no, you know, we've got debts to pay. We've got this to do, and we have that do to, and it's our money, we're going to keep it here." I think it's telling that the congregation steps out of the boundaries and is willing to do these things. . . . We seem to take things that are seemingly impossible and make them possible and there's that sense, you know . . . it's an idea and somehow we'll figure it out and we'll work it out. . . . There's faith that if it's something that's worthwhile, Christ centered, or the right thing to do, we'll find a way to do it.

They went on to tell us about a beloved grandmother in the congregation, aged one hundred, whose advice was always "Let's not worry about it. Let's just do it. It'll happen." This elder had the maturity to find courage in God's provision and the confidence to trust that when God is leading, the right things will happen.

South Valley has been around for nearly two centuries, but their orientation to risky mission is as fresh as the sunrise. They have chosen to be deliberate in their inclusion of people with differing abilities and capacities. They have embraced the courage God has given them to reach out and love those who are not like them. "Children who can't behave are welcome here," the minister told us. At-risk youth have a place in the youth programs, even though they might seem dangerous to the middle-class Euro-Canadian congregation that sponsors the programs. A person with an illness that "makes her kind of scary" to others is "included in absolutely everything. She gets invited out to stuff all the time. If people have an extra ticket [to an event], they call her and give her a ride. There are people here who are just not 'fitter-inners' for one reason or another. Yet they come." And they are welcomed. It's in South Valley's heart—their courage—as a congregation to be welcoming even of those whose differences might frighten or intimidate some middle-class, privileged folk.

Perhaps our sense of the courage of South Valley should be tempered with a sense of their deep, faithful willingness to give sacrificially. The effort to give such a sizable donation to children overseas and then add yet more money and personal labor to that effort, all at the expense of delaying the longed-for renovations to their own church building, is a remarkable story. But such willingness does not stand alone as a noteworthy, one-off achievement. In the ecosystem of such congregations, sacrificial and courageous risk manifests in a range of activities. It means meeting, welcoming, and embracing neighbors as they are. It means entering into relationships with folks around us who might never put a thin dime on the offering plate. They might never come to our Sunday morning worship services. They might never grab a seat at a Bible study. But an outreaching, self-extending, courageous—and yes, sacrificial—willingness to serve others seems closer to the spirit of Jesus Christ, whose life and ministry were all about such self-giving. It is humbling and inspiring to hear about and meet Christians like this, whose life together is important and crucial to them but who are still so beautifully committed to acts of loving service toward those who cannot necessarily reciprocate. The virtue of courage is so evident in these persons and in the way they put their faith in action. They also reveal the virtue of kenosis, which we will explore further in chapter 7.

THE VIRTUE OF COURAGE

Courage is an ancient human virtue, along with its accompanying action—risk-taking. In evolutionary terms, courageous risk was undoubtedly essential for our ancestors' survival, from hunting for food to fleeing an approaching ice age. All cultures, ancient and modern, praise courage. The brave are admired and often elevated to leadership. The title of "hero" is most often reserved for those who rise to the challenge of facing danger or hardship with courageous and selfless acts. The Bible prompts readers to cultivate courage and honors those who reveal courage in what they do. As one of the four classic cardinal virtues (together with prudence, temperance, and justice), it is part of the Christian account of a good way to live.

The hymn tradition is full of exhortations and celebrations of courage. Consider the early twentieth-century favorite "God of Grace and God of Glory":

God of grace and God of glory,
On your people pour your power.
Now fulfill your church's story,
Bring to bud its glorious flower.
Grant us wisdom, grant us courage,
For the facing of this hour.[1]

Harry Emerson Fosdick wrote this hymn in 1930 "while the United States was in the throes of the Great Depression between the two World Wars. Fosdick was a champion of the social gospel, a movement that recognized the plight of the poor."[2] He knew the gritty realities facing real people and called on them to put their trust in God and to find courage in God's sustaining presence.

One of the catchiest songs written for children's church programming has kids standing up and shout-singing, "Be strong and courageous! Do not be terrified! Do not be discouraged! For the Lord our God is with you wherever you go." This is a near-perfect paraphrase of Joshua 1:9 (and parallel passages), in which God tells Joshua not to be afraid as he leads God's people into the promised land. They had escaped slavery in Egypt; they had crossed the treacherous desert; indeed, a whole generation had passed away, including their beloved leader, Moses. Now all that remained was to enter the promised land—and to face new challenges and obstacles, all without their trusted leader and the wisdom of the elders. Like his people, Joshua wavered and was uncertain. But God said, "Be strong and courageous; do not be frightened or dismayed, for the Lord your God is with you wherever you go" (Josh 1:9).[3]

Courage is likewise the chief virtue for which Esther is remembered. In the face of the tyrannical and arbitrary power of a mercurial king and a murderous civil servant, Esther receives courage enough to confront injustice and thereby averts genocide. The Feast of Purim is still celebrated in her honor. Among many others, Joshua, Esther, David, Jael, Judith, and Gideon are remembered for their courage millennia after they lived. The same motif is picked up in the Gospel of John when Jesus bids his long farewell to his disciples. The worst of their fears was coming true. The movement they had been part of starting was being suppressed. Their hope for a new Israel and freedom from Roman oppression was vanishing before their eyes. Now their beloved leader, Jesus, was announcing that his predicted arrest and execution were about to take place—any minute. Into this chaos and confusion, this fear and anxiety, Jesus says to his followers, "Take courage; I have overcome the world" (John 16:33 NASB).

Is it enough to be *told* to have courage? Is it any different from the saccharine advice "don't worry, be happy"? Can we *will ourselves* into courage? Many of the great stories of courage in recent history seem to be grounded in individuals and groups pursuing what they know to be right, even when the odds are against them or even when they know that their inner resources feel inadequate to the task at hand. The slightly old-fashioned advice to "screw up your courage" points to how difficult this can be. It may not come naturally; rather, it has to be summoned somehow—or so it seems. A contemporary pop song called "Brave," sung by Sara Bareilles, urges listeners to exercise courage in the face of personal trouble. In contemporary social media, women and sometimes men praise and honor each other for being *brave*. It remains one of the great virtues in the cultures of Canada and the United States, even in times of relative peace and prosperity.

COURAGE AS GOD'S GIFT

In theological terms, we can locate courage within the array of gifts that God provides for the living of a good life, a life lived in God's way. The pattern to notice is that God blesses or gives spiritual gifts to persons and communities that need certain capacities for specific tasks. God gives the gifts of teaching, leadership, compassion, and care, among others, to build up the community and empower God's people to contribute to God's mission. As Paul writes, "Now there are varieties of gifts, but the same Spirit; and there are varieties of services, but the same Lord; and there are varieties of activities, but it is the same God who activates all of them in everyone. To each is given the manifestation of the Spirit for the common good" (1 Cor 12:4–7).

Courage and other gifts are not necessarily innate capacities. Courage should be located within the matrix of gifts that God gives for the strengthening of communities and the advancing of God's purposes. In other words, courage—like all God's gifts—is not given so that individuals can feel especially pleased with themselves. It is not a reward for good behavior or a badge of honor. It is not an achievement or an occasion for vanity. Indeed, many of those whom we call "heroes" in the modern era often tell the media who interview them, "I just did what anyone would do," or "I'm no one special; I just did the right thing." They don't see their courageous attitudes and actions as personal accomplishments. Courage is not given to make us beautiful or famous. It is a gift given so that God's mission in the world—God's purposes—can be further realized.

In these terms, we saw many signs of courage within our study of today's thriving communities of faith. They are willing to take risks and expose themselves to hardships and dangers of various kinds. They express courage in many ways, even when they begin a risky project or initiate a change without the reassuring confidence of success. In much of the last half of the twentieth century, mainline churches in settled, prosperous, majority-culture neighborhoods in the United States and Canada didn't have to take a lot of risks. The dominant culture and the church were mutually supportive. In many ways, it was hard to tell them apart. Children prayed the Lord's Prayer in morning assemblies in public schools. They heard a Bible story read aloud to them by their teachers. Citizenship classes were held in church halls and parlors. Christian prayers were commonly uttered within town councils and other public legislative meetings. For most of the twentieth century, Canada and the United States were still well and truly embedded in Christendom—that is, embedded in far-reaching social, cultural, and political networks in which Christianity was the normative religion and thought shaper.

In the postwar years especially, risk was not a felt experience (nor indeed required) for mainline congregations on the whole. As the civic population grew, churches were built, and the neighbors showed up. There are many anecdotes of congregations starting up in a school gym as a new suburban neighborhood was built. A denomination like the United Church of Canada would send a minister into a community, and twenty or thirty families would start up the new church plant. Within a year or two, a new sanctuary would be ready, and two hundred or three hundred people would fill it. A few years later, a Christian Education wing would be built out of durable and practical cinder blocks, painted hospital green or sunset orange, complete with a full gymnasium, several classrooms, and a kitchen.

The people of the congregation gave financially—often sacrificially—for all this to happen, but there was little doubt that these congregations would grow and flourish.

ALL IS NOT LOST

Today, as many congregations decline rapidly, their buildings are in need of significant repair. As an aging congregation struggles to pay for both a building and a minister as well as an outreaching mission, things are often much more difficult. The sense of inevitable growth and expansion is long gone. Success and even financial viability are far from guaranteed. Indeed, the survival of a given local church often appears perilous. The world around us is "VUCA"—volatile, uncertain, complex, and ambiguous.[4] This becomes so preoccupying that it is not uncommon to hear some congregations speak in distorted and obsessive ways about "the church's survival," as if the purpose of the church was to survive or to survive in a specific form. The lessons of history—that God's mission goes forward in many forms, and the church is always reinventing itself—become lost within the fog of the collective anxiety of the people and the tyranny of the church budget. The virtue of courage seems more difficult to find and to exercise.

Even so, all is not lost. Courage has not vanished—and in theological terms, God does not withhold it. We found in our study of thriving Christian communities that there are many congregations that have been inspired to "go for it." Facing many of the same grim realities as other churches, these folks, for differing reasons, have found the resolve to take some risks. This is indeed an age of decline for the mainline church. But it is also an age of chutzpah—seed-scattering, entrepreneurial, risk-taking chutzpah. Many of the Christian communities in our study have found within themselves a willingness to be vulnerable to change, not knowing in advance how things would turn out and having no control over the outcomes. Sometimes this came about at a point in their life together when it didn't seem like there was much to lose. They had already lost so much; what more could go wrong? As mentioned in chapter 2, Andrea said of Tenth Street Church, "They were a bit of a resurrection church in that they had gone through the Good Friday experience and put everything on the table and decided, 'Well, I guess that's it, we should just close the doors.'"

There had been dissension in the congregation because of a previous minister. In ways that are not immediately obvious and explainable, this was also around the same time that the congregation started to experience a resurgence. Andrea told us, "They actually faced death, and then they started to look for life again. . . . They had nothing left to lose." When new people came to the church, they were warmly welcomed, but "there wasn't a sense of desperation," as one congregant put it. They were simply and genuinely glad to say "hello" to newcomers. They didn't need to fall over themselves to get a new person onto a dying committee in order to prop it up, and they weren't desperate for that person's financial contributions. This provided a new sense of openness and gracious welcome, accepting people as they arrived and on their own terms. How, if, and when they supported the congregation were matters for another season.

RISKING FAILURE

The thriving Christian communities we got to know in our study are often willing to be wrong and unafraid to be wrong. "It's OK to fail" was the way one person summarized it. If things don't go as planned, the communities and congregations try something else instead of looking for someone or something to blame. Many ministers, priests, and congregations we know through personal contacts are apt to blame each other for forces and circumstances that are simply beyond their control. Blame is freely assigned first to a secularized society, or to Sunday shopping and sports, or to any variety of external factors. Then the blame gets shifted inwardly in the form of neurotic sniping and cannibalistic dissension. But the massive cultural shift we have experienced in the last half century—the de-Christianizing of Canada and the United States and declining interest in church participation—cannot be laid at the feet of any one congregation or minister. The habit of blaming each other for large-scale cultural shifts and the problems they have created for the church gets us stuck in a destructive rut. The "blame game" can alienate minister, people, and members of the congregation from one another. In situations like that, communities of faith have trouble being creative and imaginative. We don't have the emotional and psychic energy that is needed to learn, adapt, grow, and change. We become humorless and rigid. But Margaret Wheatley throws down a challenge: "Do we become one who does nothing but complain for what's been lost? . . . Or do we acknowledge where we are and step forward to serve?"[5]

Thriving Christian communities, in contrast, don't dwell much on failure or inadequacy. "This is a place that is not anxious about its future, even when we only have twenty-five on a Sunday," one congregation told us. They listen for how God is leading them and stay curious about what that will mean for them. They also are prepared to be patient in waiting for the Spirit to move, to change them, and to help them reach their neighbors in service and friendship. One minister said, "I am trying to let go of that stuff that's of the ego, but not of the Spirit. That's hard to know, and I'm not at all very perfect at that or anything. But this church does a good job of discernment and of listening for that Spirit. . . . We're going to go with God. That's where the energy is. We are going to look for where God is. And that might be outside [of our four walls, beyond what we are used to]." A member of that same church said, "We are consciously listening for the Spirit and [we are] willing to be led by the Spirit." This measure of openness is an expression of courage. Courage looks upon difficult circumstances and acts anyway. Courage remains open to being led rather than rigidly trying to control outcomes. Courage looks to the Holy Spirit rather than more narrowly expecting that only our human capacities are enough.

Many thriving Christian communities are also fearless in advocating for justice and inclusion, even when it is not a popular or easy stance to take in their communities. As one minister put it, "This church strives to put its faith into practice. We don't do it perfectly, but we're passionate about that." In the case of Tenth Street Church, it was a difficult but faithful decision—right at their lowest point in terms of numbers and collective energy—to offer sanctuary to a refugee family who wanted to stay in Canada when they faced deportation. The congregation, although it was fairly small, had to provide all the necessities of life and even risk running afoul of the law for this daring act of protection. As one member told us, "I'll never forget: one of the study groups we had here was about letters. It was organized around letters—Scripture letters and other letters. And I'll never forget the night we were looking at Martin Luther King Jr.'s 'Letter from a Birmingham Jail,' and I heard someone say, 'Oh, when I read this, I knew I was the white liberal' in the context of the decisions [about giving sanctuary to the refugee family], and then I said, 'I think I might go to jail now.' And I was like, 'Whoa!'" Courage can catch us by surprise, as God helps us rise to the occasion before us. It is characteristic of the gift of courage that we don't begin with abundant confidence: we begin in uncertainty, and then God begins to move in and through us. Perhaps the flip side of the coin of courage is humility.

The risk taken by Tenth Street to intervene on behalf of the refugee family seemed to spark in them a new sense of purpose, a new lease on life. Their courage and willingness to take a risk paid off in the gift of new vitality. That same church has decided now, after the period of sanctuary has ended, to invest time and energy in reaching out to a low-income housing area near their building. "There are four churches within walking distance," they told us, "and nobody spends time with them [the folks in the low-income housing]." Some of the people from the economically marginalized community have reciprocated the church's interest and now attend worship or help out with various projects. "They are really gung ho to make that happen, and they feel like they're contributing to something," we were told. The courageous risk-taking of reaching out to neighbors of a different socioeconomic class bore fruit they did not expect. Their motive was not to get "more bums in pews" but just to serve their neighbors down the street. The growth of the relationship has turned out to be a delightful result of that impetus to serve, to put faith and love into action. The courage garnered by risking much to serve refugees—perhaps even prison—translated into greater courage and resolve to serve the impoverished in their own neighborhood.

A FINAL NOTE

Aversion to courageous, faithful risk is like holding the nail while the hammer of decline comes pounding down. There is a witticism in circulation these days that asks, "What are the seven last words of the church?" (playing on the idea of Jesus's seven last words from the cross). The answer is "We've never done it that way before." As people with experience leading congregations through thick and thin, we (Russ and Rob) have literally heard it many times in council and committee meetings! It reveals an underlying apprehension that new initiatives will be risky and therefore costly, both in terms of finances and other resources. New initiatives might not work out, and that challenges the familiar, comfortable, and reliable patterns that faith communities become accustomed to—even if it is a pattern of decline and increasing decrepitude.

In contrast, the risk-taking, courageous spirit that infuses thriving congregations translates into a willingness to try out new projects, experiments, and programs without overthinking them. Thriving Christian communities tend not to balk at such risks. In fact, many of them embrace newness in the expectation that those very disruptions to the norm actually bring revived life and greater faithfulness to God's purposes. As one congregant told us,

> *I've heard a few times from different people that there's ... a spirit of willingness to try new things, and I think that people are much more willing to come forward and have ideas when they know that they're not going to get shot down. 'Cause there's lots of congregations where, if it's outside of ... any kind of box, like absolutely not. Well, that immediately shuts people down. There will be people who will never ever suggest anything ever again. But perhaps there is just a spirit of openness of trying.... "Yeah, let's try it." If it works, it works, and ...*

The unfinished sentence at the end of this person's remarks is itself suggestive of the faith community's openness to the undreamt of, the unknown, and the possible. It points toward the kind of courage given to Joshua, Esther, and the disciples of Jesus—among countless others—as they looked to God to lead them into the next phase of life. Readiness to experiment with newness frees us from the locked rooms of the predictable and expected. In the age of declining churches, it is precisely the unpredictable and unexpected that we need. It is precisely our embrace of the courage God gives that will help us step forward in faith to see what God has in store.

QUESTIONS FOR DISCUSSION

1. When you read about places like South Valley (spending their savings on classrooms in an AIDS orphanage instead of on their own

building project) or Tenth Street (giving sanctuary to refugees), how do you feel? Consider what may be behind those feelings and how they might be God nudging you forward.

2. How risk averse is your community of faith? Can you think of the last time you did something courageously risky together?

3. How is God leading you to respond to the needs in your community?

TWO CHALLENGES

1. Contact local politicians, community organizers, social workers, educators, or medical personnel and ask them what the pressing needs are in your neighborhood. Think about a project your church could develop (or partner in with others) to respond to one of those needs.

2. Set up a Bible study to learn about the acts of courageous persons in the Bible. What do they have in common? What is admirable about them? What does their example inspire in your group?

A SENSE OF IDENTITY
The Virtue of Integrity

Poplar Heights Community Church has learned that its identity is continually morphing and adjusting to the community around it. At first, after it was founded, there was a period of stability in the demographics for about thirty years. But the last twenty years have brought breathtaking change. The largely middle-class white neighborhood now has much more diversity in terms of race and ethnicity. There are two poorer neighborhoods within a thirty-minute bus ride, and folks from those communities are coming to the church more and more often. And one new subsection of the area, built on a green bluff overlooking a beautiful winding river, is populated by wealthier citizens who moved in and built "monster" homes with extra bedrooms, dens, and swimming pools. Some of those wealthier folks also like coming to Poplar Heights. Whereas once "we were all about the same," now the congregation is much more mixed, economically as well as racially. They are excited about this change in their life together. The solidly built A-frame church structure is in good repair, and its wood-and-brick exterior matches the suburban aesthetic of the split-level homes around it. The architect and builders were perhaps trying to blend into the neighborhood. But now the people are not all the same, and they don't want to be blended and have their individuality disappear. But they are eager for community and belonging, and Poplar Heights offers that.

As people come and go from the congregation, the "DNA" of the church is still Christian and focused on following Jesus, but just about everything else shifts as needed. The era in which everything was decided by the minister has given way to the present, in which (as we were told) "there's a lot of ownership from people. This is their church." They know who they are and why they are there. One person put it this way: "We are open-minded, we are evolving, we are diverse, we are Christian, we are spiritual. We make room for people whose beliefs have progressed beyond the creedal but still allow the creedal people to feel at home. We're a congregation that views itself as trying to model itself in Jesus's teaching. That manifests itself in the areas of social justice, inclusiveness, acceptance of all others . . . no matter who you are, and no matter where you are on life's journey, you're welcome here. That's what I think." The people around him nodded enthusiastically. His sense of the people of this faith community matched their sense of things as well. Another layperson chipped in, "Yes—our values focus heavily on the teachings of Jesus and trying to emulate that openness and inclusiveness." We asked if there is a biblical image that captures the spirit of their church. There was a bit of quiet reflection, then two people commented,

> I think an image that comes to my mind . . . is the woman at the well, where there's conversation, there's engagement, and at the end of the day, there was the statement that those who worship God worship God in spirit and truth. Which was a way of saying . . . that your authentic encounter with the divine is what's important. And I think that that's a kind of a baseline for us. . . . I think that . . . there is still the generation that says, "I come to church because that is what you do," and there are a number of people now that come because "this is what I choose to do." And that is not out of guilt or out of obligation, but it is out of participation and out of desire. I need something in my life that I'm not getting [in] other places. That's what I sense, anyway.

> I think we're pretty well known in the city and even in the county as a place that is very community and justice oriented. Just last year, we got the _____ award for community service. Yeah, and I think . . . a lot of people [in the neighborhood] would say that this place is a portal for their social justice work.

Poplar Heights is still changing. It's not staying still. But the sense of who they are as a diverse people is settling deeply into their bones. Newcomers and folks who are well established there are buying into the congregation's ethos and purpose. They're connected with the spiritual message they are receiving and finding outlets for service. The mixture of race and economic background is not hindering them but enriching who they are and making them even more accessible and inviting to their neighbors. They are experiencing and demonstrating the virtue of *integrity*, by which we mean not only an ethical standard but also the concept of being *integrated*. Who they are and what they do are integrated, not just in sermons or formal organizational documents, but across the broad spectrum of the congregation's population—in their hearts and their heads.

Most of the thriving Christian communities that we met and interviewed in our research consistently have a strong sense of identity. They know *who* they are, *why* they are, and *where* they are going. A range of experiences and structural features within their life together as "church" has the effect of binding them together more closely than a crowd of strangers ever can be. Relationships have been built up over time, and there is often a sense of cohesiveness about their reason for being. In other words, they have a shared purpose, and they are linked together through that purpose. Undergirding all of this is a strong sense of their faith foundations: they are the people of God, followers of Jesus, sharing a community that is committed to seeking and living out God's intentions for the world. These features combine in a powerful way, as we saw with Poplar Heights. Even so, the landscape of each faith community is different. There is no "one size fits all" way to describe these churches and their people. It would be a mistake to try to offer a general profile of *the* identity of a thriving congregation or some kind of ideal. Instead, in this chapter, we'll explore a number of themes that relate to the integrity of identity and share what our interviewees told us about what it means for them to be who they are.

COVENANT

The Bible has some important things to say about the identity of communities of faith. In the First Testament, the whole of Israel is often regarded as a single people whose faith, nationhood, and identity are all intertwined as "God's chosen." All of this is grounded, of course, in the powerful covenant that God makes with Israel. As God promises to Jacob (whose name will later become *Israel*), "Know that I am with you and will keep you wherever you go" (Gen 28:15). Different versions of this covenant are made with Noah, Abraham and Sarah, Moses and Miriam, and the whole of Israel, and God's covenant is renewed again and again in Israel's story. One of its most beautiful expressions is found in Isaiah 49:15–16:

> Can a woman forget her nursing child,
>   or show no compassion for the child of her womb?
> Even these may forget,
>   yet I will not forget you.
> See, I have inscribed you on the palms of my hands.

And again in Isaiah 54:10:

> For the mountains may depart
>   and the hills be removed,
> but my steadfast love shall not depart from you,
>   and my covenant of peace shall not be removed,
>   says the Lord, who has compassion on you.

It is incredible to realize that these and other reassurances of God's presence and care are offered not when everything is going great, with roses and bread and gentle rains for everyone. God makes these promises precisely during a time of national chaos and distress (the exile in Babylon). Churches experiencing distress and worry in our time and place might be helped in remembering that dynamic. In the everlasting covenant, God chooses Israel and indeed all of creation, holding them in an eternal embrace of love.

Within this heritage of trust and inexhaustible love, the testimony of Jesus finds its place. He speaks of a "new covenant" when he shares the Last Supper with his disciples. He reassures his hearers that his ministry and witness stand in continuity with God's eternal embrace of Israel: "Do not think that I have come to abolish the law or the prophets; I have come not to abolish but to fulfill" (Matt 5:17). Zechariah, the old man who gratefully greeted the child Jesus in the temple, saw this as well: "Thus [God] has shown the mercy promised to our ancestors, and has remembered [the] holy covenant" (Luke 1:72). Paul and other Second Testament authors similarly locate the significance of Jesus and the new movement that emerged in his name within the covenant. As the writer of Hebrews puts it, "He [Jesus] is the mediator of a new covenant, so that those who are called may receive the promised eternal inheritance" (Heb 9:15). The ancient covenants of God with Israel, renewed in and through Jesus, are the foundation of the Christian community's identity in its earliest and subsequent years. Christianity did not appear out of thin air: it was always a branch of the family tree, so to speak, that had already been growing for thousands of years. The rich soil that roots and nourishes that tree is the covenant that God offers and promises to all generations.

In theological terms, this covenantal relationship with God underlies the identity of all faith communities. God has claimed us and called us beloved. We are invited into an international commonwealth that cuts across space and time—the Kingdom or Community of Heaven. As those who are "inscribed on the palms of God's hands," we are never outside the care and concern of God. Congregations today can rely and lean back on that promise. God's love sustains and guides us, always.

COMMUNITY AND KINSHIP

Today, the covenant love and embrace of God are experienced in many ways, including the sacrament of Baptism. The Christian practice of Baptism has, as one of its meanings, the welcome of a person into the household of God, the body of Christ. This sacrament says, among other things, that we belong to God, and we belong to each other. As Paul puts it, "Whether we live or whether we die, we are the Lord's" (Rom 14:8). Baptism reasserts the ancient covenant again and again and is one of the most visible signs we offer, celebrating that membership in the church—the community of faith—runs deeper than and is far more significant than joining a club. No one "must" join the church, but participating in the life of the church and choosing active membership reflects our embrace of God's embrace of us, and it starts to change who we are at a deep level. This deep choosing of their faith community (as we heard from the folks at Poplar Heights at the beginning of this chapter) strengthens who they are together. Sharing and participating in the life of the faith community reinforces that deep identity. We're not simply carbon atoms bouncing around the planet: We are covenant people. We are bound to one another and to God in a profound and transformative way. By being church, we become family. We are not blood relations, but our kinship is deep, strong, and significant. The phrase "all my relations," which is often said when Indigenous speakers address a group, perhaps points in this direction as well. It recognizes our deep connectedness to one another, to creation, and to the Creator.

In the church community, kinship in and through Christ and the Creator turns strangers into friends. We are bound together in a greater whole, a wider identity than mere individuals. Our individuality is not erased, but "individual" is not the only definition of who we are. In the thriving congregations we met, we often heard this expressed in terms of inclusivity and breadth of imagination. There is little mention of words like "outsiders," "nonmembers," or other terms that distinguish the church community from their neighbors. Rather, there is scope and openness that permit embrace and encounter. The local church is not perceived as a retreat or hiding place from the wider world. The church (which is the people, after all) is set within the wider world, part of it, dynamically interacting with it on a daily basis. Grace Church in chapter 2 was an amazing example of this. The church is the body of Christ, without a doubt, but that body lives and moves and acts within a context, among neighbors and friends and strangers, serving and honoring them, discovering their needs and joys. "We don't have an organ. We don't even have a piano. Just a keyboard," one church told us. "We are never going to be the church that's known for the chancel choir and the handbell choir, right? That's never going to be us. . . . But we are really good at Vacation Bible School. . . . One of our strengths is ministry to children and youth. Huge resources are poured into [these programs] including a significant proportion [offered to] families we never see [in worship] and never get a nickel from." There is a clear shift in thriving congregations away from being an ark that floats above the floodwaters of the world toward being an oceangoing vessel that explores the wide world and welcomes on board any who wish to explore its decks or help trim the sail. As a wise person once said, nearly one hundred years ago, "A ship in harbor is safe, but that is not what ships are built for."[1] In other words, mission in, for, and with the community around the church is close to the heart of the identity of thriving congregations. It gives them integrity because they are *of* the people around them, not a club set apart from them.

COHESIVENESS

A related feature of the identities of thriving communities of faith is their sense of cohesiveness. This varies, of course, and not every person necessarily feels well integrated or part of the action. But we found that most of the people we interviewed express a strong feeling that their life together is closely aligned with their overall sense of purpose and of who they are as a local congregation. Purpose is very much at the heart of their sense of identity. They sometimes speak of it in terms of being part of something larger. As one interviewee said, "That [feeling of] meaning comes from devoting yourself to something that you may or may not call duty." The language is "we" and "us" language, not making sharp distinctions between different groups within the congregation, nor between congregation and minister. These folks' sense of purpose strengthens and reinforces their trust in God and in each other. In fact, trusting God in some cases helps them see what their larger purpose is all about. In other words, they don't spend much time sitting at a board meeting table wondering what their purpose should be.

As our colleague Christine Jerrett once said, the conversations in thriving congregations shift from "How do we fix the church?" to "What is God up to?"[2] That outward orientation—what we name in this book as *turning ourselves inside out*—helps us move our unproductive attention away from our own problems and struggles so that we can notice and follow where God is at work in the world (see chapter 7). That doesn't mean we neglect the roof if it's leaking, but it does mean that we resist becoming obsessive about repairs. It doesn't mean that we forget about making sure there are kids' program leaders ready to welcome children on Sundays, but it does mean that we also save some energy for reflection and response to the movement of the Holy Spirit in the community and world around us. If we are truly followers of Jesus, and people who are letting God lead us through life, then we have to give meaningful attention to what God is up to. One minister told us, "I think that the Spirit is at work . . . and a big part of our job is listening for that. We're going to go with God, where the energy is. We are going to look for where God is. And that's outside [the four walls of the building]." The life of the church isn't limited to what we know and are already doing.

Here's where the rubber hits the road: we (Russ and Rob) are convinced that God is not leading the church into preserving and perpetuating the status quo. The status quo is leading to decline in most faith communities. When decline has happened before in Christian history, God disrupts and reorients the faithful toward new ways of being. The constant refrain among mainline Christians that "the church is in decline" is mostly a cipher for "my preferred version of the church is declining." Yet God is doing new things if we have the eyes to see them! Thriving congregations don't embody an identity of decline. They embody an identity of hopeful expectation about what God can do. They are not just optimistic: they are "all ears" about what the Spirit might want to whisper to them. God is in the lead.

Cohesiveness as a Christian community often emerges as a result of working together. It might be a special project, or a time-limited task, or an ongoing service responsibility or mission. Even cooking a meal together, sitting down to eat, having a good conversation, and then cleaning up the dishes will help form stronger bonds. In a society in which a huge proportion of people eat their meals alone each day, simply sharing a meal is a significant act both of resistance to human isolation and of encouraging community building. In being together, we remind each other that we are not alone. Jesus is a strong example of a God-filled person who loved to share meals with friends and strangers. He enjoyed a party, so much so that his critics accused him of being a glutton and a drunkard (Luke 7:34). He ate with the lovely and the unlovely, the clean and the unclean, the socially acceptable and the rejects. The way of Jesus is still a way that leads to life. His radically inclusive/disruptive approach can inspire and transform our communities if we are prepared to risk trying that approach. "There is horrific need," we were told, in a community next to one of the churches we interviewed. "And it's not just poverty; it's addiction and abuse and all the ancillaries." In response, that rural congregation decided to take a turn once a month to provide a free community supper to anyone who needs it. Other churches and local groups also take a turn. "It's the same food you'd have to pay for at a church [fundraising] dinner," their minister told us. "It's shepherd's pie or roast beef or roast turkey and all the vegetables and homemade pies and nice buns. A woman here says, 'If it's good enough to sell, it's good enough to give away.'" Their collective efforts and donations of food and money from within the congregation make this generous and tasty meal happen every month, without fail. Their readiness to help their neighbors springs from their identity but also reinforces their identity: *this is who we are*. The same church built an addition with lots of volunteer labor, goes on mission trips together to dig wells, and recently funded and welcomed a refugee family into their community.

Cohesiveness within thriving faith communities is also revealed in a congregation's shared sense of integrity. That is, they are able to say *this is who we are, and we know that to be true about us, so this is why we do what we do*. Their shared identity permeates who they are and the actions they take. There is a high degree of ownership and consensus about these matters. It is not only the minister who is expected to articulate the church's identity and mission. Many members, or even most, can say clearly why the congregation exists and what they are doing to express their purpose. This isn't quite the same as a congregation saying what it believes in the sense of doctrinal claims. It has more to do with the deep missional DNA that sustains them. To return to the sailing metaphor, these are congregations that know the kind of ship they are on, how to sail it, and where it is headed.

This kind of integrity and shared identity is not developed overnight. It takes many months and even years to take shape. It does mean spending some time to come to a consensus about purpose and mission. But that period of discernment and reflection can't come to a stop once a "mission statement" is written and posted on the wall or stuck in a file among an archive of meeting minutes. In fact, we (Russ and Rob) suggest that you don't agonize about writing a mission statement for your church. Skip that completely. Too many churches write mission statements then forget about them, or tie up countless hours arguing about the wording only to find that no one remembers what it actually says. Focus instead on *embodying the mission and taking action*. Who you are as a church and what you are up to together need discussion, but they need action too. The missional purpose of a congregation crystallizes only after the work of mission is engaged. It is in *doing* the things we feel called to do as a community (and not just talking about what should be done) that we discover the integrity of shared purpose. Margaret Wheatley, a management consultant and systems analyst, says, "It's not strategic plans . . . that create change. We need to see clearly the narrative we are blindly following and consciously choose the storyline of who we want to become."[3]

FAITH FOUNDATIONS

For many of those we interviewed, the faith foundations of their lives and churches are central to their identity. Among United Church of Canada people (probably the most liberal main cohort within our study), open and enthusiastic expressions of personal faith are not as common as they are in some other church traditions. So for some of the folks we interviewed, this aspect of life is somewhat muted. But for others, their visible expressions and joyful experiences of faith are clearly key to who they are and why they live the way they do. They identify as Christians and as followers of Jesus. As one interviewee said, "We preach Jesus every single Sunday. . . . Our experiences of Christ are talked about here." They are the people of God and members of a local church. These identity markers are core to how they understand themselves as human beings set within creation and their own contexts. As one congregation put it, "We're passionate about being disciples and followers." Another church told us that they are "a third member of the Trinity kind of church," meaning that they are strongly connected to the Holy Spirit.

These faith foundations prove to be trustworthy and helpful to thriving congregations because faith helps them steer away from anxiety about their church's survival. Their sense of the everyday goodness and long-term presence and faithfulness of God helps them to risk the security of the status quo and try new things without knowing in advance how it will all turn out. Survival, which seems to be the focus of so many churchy conversations these days, is not something these folks are focused on, because they believe that survival is not the purpose of the church. Christianity doesn't exist simply to survive. The purpose is to be God's people, loving and serving our communities and the world.

John Bell, the internationally renowned musician and preacher from the Iona Community in Scotland, tells the story of a Uniting Church congregation in Australia with about thirty worshippers, all over the age of sixty-five. Their new part-time minister asked them what was next in their life together. What did they want for their future? They assumed she would advise them to close down. But she didn't. She waited for them to speak their hearts. One fellow suggested they really should close down since they were located in an industrial area with no real housing in the area. With faithful daring, they struck out in a new direction as they talked it over for a few weeks. The conversations flowed like this: "Maybe we could get money for the building. . . . And then what? . . . We could build a new church. . . . Why build another? There are plenty of churches. . . . There is a house in the area, part social housing, part private housing. We could go there and [rent] the community center." Bell asked a congregation member to tell him what happened next, and she told him,

> We shut the church and sold it, then opened up in the community cen-
> ter. We don't open on Sunday morning at 11:00; we meet on Wednes-
> day night at 6:30. We don't begin with a praise band or with an organ
> playing—we begin with a meal for an hour. Then we spend about an
> hour and a half in worship, in different ways than we've ever done before,
> and we close at about 9:00 or 9:15. When we moved there, we had about
> 30 people, and after two years we've got 110, many of whom have never
> been to church before. Let me tell you, John: These are the happiest hours
> I've ever spent in church in my life.

It turns out that this person was the organist from the old building and was eighty-three years of age. Bell concludes, "This is a vocation we have to encourage in congregations who think they are 'past it.' They *can* do new things."[4] The faith foundations of this older, mature congregation gave them the strength of purpose to launch into something entirely new. They were prepared to plant seeds in new soil and wait on God to see what the growth would be.

One critique of this aspect of identity (faith foundations) could be that all Christian faith communities "should" always have their faith on display, front and center, loud and proud, and top of mind in all aspects of their life together. Faith "should" be the first thing they talk about and build on. In one sense, this is true. Faith communities are unlike other social groupings in this very real way. The free and open expression of faith is often deeply strengthening for Christians, and it does have a rightful place in a congregation's life together. One of our interviewees concludes that being too low-key about our faith foundations might be a mistake: "We start great ministries and then, as liberal churches, we apologize for our faith and kind of back off from that. . . . I think we screwed up when we went and apologized for being people of faith."

Talking about their foundations of faith in God was somewhat muted for a number of our interviewees. However, we don't see this as a fatal flaw. Indeed, it might be a failing in the kind of questions we asked them as interviewers or how we shaped the conversations. On the other hand, the lack of open and emotive expressions of faith is partly a feature of Canadian society in the twenty-first century, in which spirituality has become a largely private and internalized dimension of life. Recent folk wisdom suggests that by making "politics and religion" unwelcome conversation topics in social settings, Canadians have become less articulate and discerning about politics and religion. People in the United States are often more forthcoming about this topic, mind you.

Perhaps the most important thing to note on this topic is that the less extroverted nature of faith and spirituality among our research participants has not prevented them from becoming vibrant, dynamic, and outward-reaching communities of faith. That core of faith in God is still there, even if it is not talked about as much as one might expect. It is a deep well from which people draw to nourish their life together and their action in the world. Nourishing a congregation's foundations of faith pays dividends, as we saw in chapter 3.

RELATIONSHIPS

Finally, the nature of relationships in thriving communities of faith is a distinctive aspect of their identity. They have the usual struggles over space and money, authority and decision-making. There are still personality conflicts. But they have a sense (as noted above) of being kin to each other, people on a journey who are interconnected through the loving presence and purposes of God. As we were told, "I want the church to be a place where people's spirituality is deepened, where we learn to love one another, love ourselves, and love God." They tend to see their congregation not as a collection of individuals but as a body or even a movement. Their relationships with their ministers tend to be warm and respectful but not necessarily deferential. The ministers, too, want a flattening of hierarchical structures. One minister told us, "I want the people here to feel connected to each other and feel a sense of life and responsibility to this community. It's not all about the preacher." The minister and people are understood as being part of the same team, pulling in the same direction. This results in a strong bond between them: "It sounds kind of corny, but I really love these people, right? Before I start my sermon, I actually pause after I've said the prayer for illumination. I actually pause, and I actually look at everybody and remind myself that I care about these people. . . . I am engaging in relationship to be changed by them as much as to change them, you know? . . . I do believe that we need each other. I believe that we are actually made that way, that it's part of how God made us."

The relationship of thriving congregations with their surrounding communities is often distinctive as well. Nonmembers and nonattenders of the church are seen not as people who "ought to care about the church" but as neighbors and possibly people who can benefit from the service and care of the church. The identity of the thriving church in this respect, then, is as a hub of activity and service for the good of the community: "This is a place that looks outward. It looks and seeks to serve the community, and . . . finds meaning in life in that." Whether or not their neighbors participate in church life is not a prime concern. Nonparticipating neighbors are not judged or resented for their indifference to the church. At the same time, interaction between church and community has a spiritual impact: "While we meet those concrete needs [of community members] . . . we also invite people to learn about each other, deepen their own sense of spirituality, and live meaningful lives." One congregation speaks of wanting to be "involved in engaging and building relationships with the world around them, [and] it's not just the minister doing that."

Last but not least—and we found this to be quite an interesting discovery—the relationship of thriving congregations with their denominational structures is not prominent in their life together. They might or might not perceive their denominational identity as important. Some of those we interviewed (ministers and laypeople) proudly claimed their denominational heritage and involvement, but most did not. The denominational relationship was something like background radiation: it was part of the story but not uppermost in their minds.

CONCLUSION

Covenant and community. Kinship and cohesiveness. Faith foundations and relationships. All of these are aspects of the identity of thriving congregations. Such congregations tend to know *who* they are and, just as importantly, *why* they are. A strong sense of purpose was a strong current running through all of our conversations. No doubt it took time for these faith communities to develop and become aware of that purpose. By the limited nature of our study, we probably didn't meet members of those churches who don't feel the same way. But these themes of a strong identity resurfaced again and again in our research, and it became clear that this was a distinctive characteristic of thriving churches. We believe that their clear sense of identity is a significant reason that they are as strong and effective as they are in starting with "yes!," taking risks, focusing on spiritual growth, embracing leadership, and turning themselves inside out.

QUESTIONS FOR DISCUSSION

1. How would you state your congregation's purpose? How well do you think your faith community can identify its purpose? Are you talking about this purpose from time to time and actively embodying it in your life together?

2. Can you see signs that your congregation's purpose is changing or that it is different than it used to be? What steps could be taken to discern whether God is leading you in a new way?

3. What can you do to get to know each other well? How can you get to know and serve your neighbors with love and care for their well-being, not just because you want them to "join" or to give your congregation money?

TWO CHALLENGES

1. In a small group setting, talk about the four to five key things that make your community of faith what it is. Avoid making a long list. Then make some posters (homemade is fine) and put them up around your building or your community to announce and remind folks who you are.

2. Spend two or three sessions in prayer with a few other people and focus on where God might be leading you. Reflect on how your community has changed (within the church and beyond it). Ask God to reveal how you can respond to those changes faithfully.

WILLINGNESS TO BE TURNED INSIDE OUT
The Virtue of Kenosis

Russ had a deeply formative experience some years ago that dissolved his understanding of God's church and left him in an open space with only intimations of how he might come to see the church going forward. This happened in 2009, at the 40th General Council of the United Church of Canada. General Council was the triennial meeting of the United Church's highest decision-making body. Hundreds of clergy and lay representatives from across the country gathered for about a week to worship, engage in visioning, and do the business of the denomination. That year, General Council took place in the dusty hills of British Columbia's Okanagan Valley. As a delegate, Russ experienced a week of meetings, presentations, worship services, and lively conversations during coffee breaks and over end-of-the-day beers.

Slowly, it dawned on him that the United Church of Canada was not one church but two. These two churches were intertwined like strands of DNA, dancing with each other, each taking the lead for a while and then giving way to the other. One partner in the dance was the denomination many had come to know over the previous nine decades since it was founded in 1925: an institutional church that had served Canada well; governed itself capably in congregations, presbyteries, and conferences; had sent thousands of personnel into mission overseas and to the needy at home; had offered strong, comforting, recognizable worship; and had cared for millions of souls, from cradle to grave. The other partner in the dance was more irregular and volatile in its movements, darting in and out of sight, harder to see but at least as strong in its presence. At that moment of history, it was a denomination more of deconstruction than of construction. It was guerrilla church. When you thought you had it in your sights, it packed up and ran out of view.

FROM TEMPLE TO TENT

Reflecting on his perception of these two different churches, Russ later came to realize that what he had witnessed in British Columbia—and what those of us in the mainline church have been witnessing for a half century—was precisely the opposite of a crucial moment in the history of ancient Israel: the inauguration of institutional religion. That moment is captured in 1 Kings 8:1–14:

> Then Solomon assembled the elders of Israel and all the heads of the tribes, the leaders of the ancestral houses of the Israelites, before King Solomon in Jerusalem, to bring up the ark of the covenant of the Lord out of the city of David, which is Zion. All the people of Israel assembled to King Solomon at the festival in the month Ethanim, which is the seventh month. And all the elders of Israel came, and the priests carried the ark. So they brought up the ark of the Lord, the tent of meeting, and all the holy vessels that were in the tent; the priests and the Levites brought them up. King Solomon and all the congregation of Israel, who had assembled before him, were with him before the ark, sacrificing so many sheep and oxen that they could not be counted or numbered. Then the priests brought the ark of the covenant of the Lord to its place, in the inner sanctuary of the house, in the most holy place, underneath the wings of the cherubim. For the cherubim spread out their wings over the place of the ark, so that the cherubim made a covering above the ark and its poles. The poles were so long that the ends of the poles were seen from the holy place in front of the inner sanctuary; but they could not be seen from outside; they are there to this day. There was nothing in the ark except the two tablets of stone that Moses had placed there at Horeb, where the Lord made a covenant with the Israelites, when they came out of the land of Egypt. And when the priests came out of the holy place,

a cloud filled the house of the Lord, so that the priests could not stand to minister because of the cloud; for the glory of the Lord filled the house of the Lord. Then Solomon said, "The Lord has said that he would dwell in thick darkness. I have built you an exalted house, a place for you to dwell in forever." Then the king turned around and blessed all the assembly of Israel, while all the assembly of Israel stood.

This passage from the First Testament describes the consolidation of institutionalized religion in ancient Israel. It is a moment of great empowerment for the people of Israel, their priests (especially), and their king. This was a people who had lived as slaves in Egypt, wandered for generations in the desert, fought a brutal war to wrestle Palestine from the nations inhabiting it, then spent centuries warding off attacks, struggling to keep its religion pure, and suffering from weak leadership. Now there is a strong king, who inherited the throne from his strong father, David. Now riches pour into Israel instead of pouring out of it. Now it is the surrounding nations that fear the sword of Israel. Centuries of chaos have given way to a time of peace and prosperity. For ages, the Israelites were a people of tents who worshipped in tents. No longer. Today they move the Ark of the Covenant from the tent into the temple. Today their God has a strong house. Today they establish a religious center from which grace will pour out over the land. The thousands who gathered that day on the dusty slope of Mount Zion witnessed a time of chaos giving way to a time of order.

For decades, the mainline church in Canada and the United States has been experiencing the opposite movement: from order to chaos, from temple to tents. What was once orderly, predictable, and well governed is now disorderly, unpredictable, and ungovernable. At the General Council meeting in 2009, tent church was especially apparent in worship. It came into view as the worship leaders borrowed symbols from diverse traditions: prayer flags from Tibetan Buddhism, prayers in the four directions from Indigenous elders, heartbreaking drama from the theatre of the oppressed. Tent church was given a face and heart by the growing leadership of the nonmajority church—Indigenous peoples, youth, Francophones, Asian and African Canadians, and the LGBTQ+ community. The denomination had gone from not listening to these people, to listening to them with paternalistic patience, to listening to them—starting at last to listen, at least—with hunger for their wisdom and their trial-tested strength. Russ came away with an enduring image of tent church imprinted on his mind's eye: a ten-year-old Asian Canadian girl who darted in and out of the meeting space, on and off of the stage throughout the week. She blessed the court with singing and acting, with gentle words and uncanny smiles, with grace and confidence.

The history of religion, the history of humankind's relations with spirit, is an interplay of order and chaos. Usually, humans don't like chaos much. We like to fix things, to solve things. But chaos is an essential element of cosmos and creation. We learn this from the opening two verses of the Bible: "In the beginning when God created the heavens and the earth, the earth was a formless void and darkness covered the face of the deep, while a wind from God swept over the face of the waters" (Gen 1:1–2). Quantum physicists teach us that when a system is marked by extreme randomness, it can mysteriously produce ordered behavior after a period of time.

To read through the First and Second Testaments and the history of the church is to find a rhythm. There is movement into structured, institutional religion; then dissolution into dynamic change and uncertainty; and then, again, the signs of an emerging new order. Solomon's time was a time of order. Our time is one of disorder. The Spirit is in the chaos right now. It has become like a solvent, pouring itself over the temple, dissolving the mortar between the stones, sending the people into tents. It takes more faith to live in times like ours. It is easier to have faith during times of growing order, when things are coming together and when the church is confident and celebrated by society. Yet if we look back at our faith history, all of the seminal figures were people who saw the faith through chaos, danger, and uncertainty: Dorothy Day, Martin Luther King Jr., Martin Luther, Peter, Mary, Ruth, Moses and Miriam, Abraham and Sarah. All of these, many more, and their communities navigated chaos with trust and hope.

GOD HAS LEFT THE BUILDING

Like many ministers, we (Russ and Rob) have spent long hours feeling frustrated and discouraged over the state of the church—a lot of time longing for the days when pews were full, when Sunday schools were bursting, when ministers had social legitimacy. In our denomination's history, there was a time in which the moderator of the United Church of Canada could call the prime minister of Canada out of the blue, and the call would be taken! We've hated the times of feeling like a chaplain to a long, slow, unstoppable decline. It seemed as though God, like Elvis, had left the building.

Now we realize that God *has* left the building in a real way. But what we couldn't see in our hours of despair was God waiting at the doorway, holding out a tent, and saying, "Go into the world. Go, and find me there. Go meet the Muslim and the Buddhist and the atheist, and you will find me there. Go meet the women and children in a shelter, and you will find me there. Go sojourn with Indigenous peoples, and you will find me there. March with Black Lives Matter, and you will find me there." Like many in the mainline, we have been slow to wake up to this. For a half century, there has been a progressive emptying of the mainline church. It is time to accept that *God is present in the emptying.* After herculean efforts to stem the flow, after decades of denial, after countless attempts to entice the populace back into our temples, after innumerable programmatic reforms, it is time to take seriously the possibility that God desires this great emptying. It is time to ask if there isn't something sacred about the deep humbling of the liberal church. It is time to consider the possibility that this is a kenosis, a self-emptying for the good of others.

Elm Avenue Church is a congregation that finds itself at the nexus of interplay between temple church and tent church. It was built as a temple: founded well over a century ago by the establishment class of a city that was then a regional center and is even more so today. Over the decades, its pews have been graced by many of the most powerful and educated citizens of the city. It has long been known for excellent music and strong sermons preached from a high pulpit. The preachers were always male. Until Stacy was hired.

The selection of Stacy was a surprise to many inside and outside the congregation. Elm Avenue Church's senior ministers always had been well-educated white men, usually tall with big personalities. They were prime examples of what was once called "muscular Christianity." Their sermons were long and scholarly. They were engaged in the larger community from a place of prestige. They were advocates of ambitious programs of charity, but they seldom critiqued the political and economic systems that undergirded their privilege. Stacy is not cut from this cloth. She is white and well educated, but she grew up working class, and her ministry was mostly spent in inner-city missions with those being crushed by the forces of marginalization.

Stacy was hired in the apparent downslope of the congregation's decline. Elm Avenue Church's story was far from over, but it was weakening. Attendance was slipping, debts were growing, prestige was waning, and the young adults who had grown up in the church were leaving en masse. Some of them simply felt that the church was not relevant. Others were frustrated with the church's homogeneity: almost everyone in the pews was white, and everyone seemed to be straight. Many saw hypocrisy in the church's charity to poor people while its members benefited from the very systems that broke the backs of the poor. Anxiety was growing into real tension, and the ministers and lay leaders were frequently falling into feuds. The group of church leaders tasked with hiring a new senior minister was looking for someone with a clear vision. Stacy definitely had one. They also were looking for someone who could respond to the criticisms of younger members. They knew that the first female senior minister would have a hard time, but Stacy appeared to be more than tough enough to handle that.

Stacy was a little surprised when she was offered the job. Friends said to her, "You're going to have one hell of a time preaching liberation theology and advocating for justice at Elm Ave." But she knew that there was a small group of social justice warriors in the congregation; she had met them at marches and mission sites. They were telling her, "Come over to us. We're primed for a real change." Stacy spent most of her first year at Elm Avenue listening and watching. She visited a lot. She organized sharing circles to draw members into deep listening and visioning. She supported a group of lay leaders who carried out a program of Appreciative Inquiry.[1] The social justice warriors got impatient with her. They had waited decades, and they wanted dramatic efforts to confront oppression organized right away. Stacy was more careful. She knew that she needed to build up trust with the membership. She knew that she would have to do a lot of listening before most folks would be ready to listen to her. And she knew that she needed more allies than just those advocating for social justice. (Later in this chapter, we will explore Otto Scharmer's concept of "presencing"—a blending of sensing and presence that allows a person or a group to "connect from the Source of the highest future possibility and bring it into the now."[2] Stacy does not use Scharmer's language, but her year of listening reveals the same activity of presencing, for herself and for her faith community.)

When the year of listening was reaching its end, members of Elm Avenue Church were expressing the very things Stacy perceived:

> *By God, we are white! Why are we not more welcoming to people of color? I think the young people are leaving because they see movements and organizations out there in the world that actually make a difference in people's lives. They don't just give them a meal or pay their power bill.*

> *I always feel afraid when I read that Jesus said "the first shall be last, and the last shall be first," because I know we are the first. I really think we should be doing something to challenge the powers that be, but I just don't know what to do. Who can teach us what to do?*

GETTING THE CHURCH OUTSIDE THE BUILDING

A core group of leaders emerged within Elm Avenue Church who felt they knew what to do. This group included Stacy and some of the social justice warriors, but they were not the majority. They had a key insight: Their job was not to go out and try to fix the world. Fixing things was too much a part of the colonial project. Their job was to build relationships with people of other races, faiths, sexual identities, and cultures. Their job was to listen to them as carefully as they had been listening to each other for the past year. Someone remembered Kirk, Spock, and Bones from the 1960s *Star Trek* television show and said, "We need to form away teams. We need to get off the mother ship and explore the world out there of people unlike ourselves." These teams were formed, they grabbed their tents, and they set out. Some spent time on meditation cushions with Buddhists. Some were invited to talking circles and ceremonies and eventually even sweat lodges with Indigenous people in the city and, later on, at reserves outside the city. Some worked to build a relationship with a Black church. They attended their worship services, organized meals and concerts for the two congregations, and arranged for pulpit swaps. Others began to volunteer at the missions where Stacy had worked, sojourning with homeless folks, serving breakfast, or just shooting the breeze over coffee and games of cards. Some developed relationships with the local mosque and joined efforts to combat Islamophobia. Some spent time in dialogue with atheists.

In those places, they found God—the God of tents.

God was in the encounter. God was in the talking circle at the moment when they realized that all peoples, Indigenous and white, were being held by the same Creator and blessed by the same Spirit. God was in the conversation when an "away team" and a Buddhist group understood that they were being called to work together on climate change. God was in the song when the Elm Avenue Church choir and a choir of street people began performing together. God was in the circle when, in the wake of the terrible killings at two mosques in Christ Church, New Zealand, members of Elm Avenue helped to form a symbolic ring of protection around a nearby mosque during Friday prayers. God was in the angry feet and voices when white people of all ages joined in protests after the killing of black men by white police officers. It was as if, through all of these encounters, the Holy Spirit was pouring solvent over the temple that Elm Avenue had been, causing it to collapse. It was not the physical temple that was falling but rather the more stubborn one—the psychological one.

For most of a decade, the two activities mentioned above—presencing and exploring in "away teams"—characterized the life of Elm Avenue. And then God reentered the physical temple and asked, "What would happen if you turned this place into a big tent?" Elm Avenue had carried on almost all of the usual activities of a mainline congregation over that decade: worship services, church board and committee meetings, study groups of various kinds, church suppers, youth group, Sunday school, and so on. But all of these activities came to be shaped more and more by the twin ventures of deep listening in adaptive conversations[3] (or presencing) and relationship building across the lines of race, religion, sexual identity, and culture. The congregation's core identity and sense of mission were changing. Yet after ten years of this, a kind of ennui was starting to set in. The actual demographic makeup of the congregation had not changed that much. There was a growing feeling that to be able to embrace its emerging future, the emptying out of Elm Avenue's old way of being needed to go further.

A more complete entry into presencing, fully shared with partners outside the church, was needed. With the help of some consultants and a couple of retreat directors who worked at the intersection of spiritual practice and social justice, Elm Avenue Church and its partner communities took a deep dive for about a year and emerged with a new vision. The vision had a name: the Interfaith Network for Reconciliation and Justice (INRJ). Elm Avenue Church and its partners (which now included mosques, synagogues, Buddhist and Hindu groups, Indigenous leaders, LGBTQ+ support groups, and a number of NGOs and social enterprises) would create a new organization that would use Elm Avenue's building as its primary physical center. As envisioned, the INRJ would place itself at the intersection of social justice and spirituality, offering dialogue processes between Indigenous people and settlers, antiracist education, interfaith dialogue opportunities, multiple programs of spiritual practice (ranging from Buddhist meditation to contemplative prayer to mindfulness), services for refugees, and leadership programs designed to bring together emerging leaders from communities historically isolated by the barriers of race, culture, class, and religion.

In addition, the INRJ would organize an annual conference for progressive leaders and change makers throughout the city and the region. This conference would work to educate and train people in the ventures mentioned above as well as systems change, community-based economics, and grassroots democracy.

GIVING UP (OR TAKING BACK) CONTROL

Elm Avenue Church remained a largely white and privileged congregation on Sunday morning, but it was about to become much more diverse for the other six and a half days of the week. As this vision was tested with the congregation, the response was positive. It felt right. It felt like a calling, even though church members knew it meant giving up some of their power. It was clear that the INRJ could not be controlled by Elm Avenue Church alone, that its governing board would have to be made up of people from a wide range of communities and organizations, and that Elm Avenue would have to surrender some control of its property. That felt right for most church members—though not all. And so the work of organizing this ambitious venture was begun. Grants were applied for and received. Partner communities contributed as much funding as they could muster. The work began well.

Before long, however, resistance started to arise within Elm Avenue Church. The first sign of trouble occurred when Stacy and a couple of members of the INRJ board organized a series of workshops for Elm Avenue members on systemic racism and allyship. The workshops were well attended but not by key church leaders or the core group of members who seemed to show up for every faith formation opportunity. Stacy started to prepare the congregation for the arrival of the INRJ and the diverse group of people who would be moving through the building by speaking of the INRJ's programs in worship and showing a lot of photos on PowerPoint. Pushback began. After one sermon that focused on reparations for the historical oppression of Black people, a white member of the church began loudly swearing at Stacy while she was shaking hands at the back of the sanctuary. Members of the church board (all white) began saying things like, "I'm not sure we can really afford to turn this place over to the INRJ," and "I don't see the financial sustainability here." A growing number in the congregation started to characterize the INRJ as "Stacy's project," forgetting the deep conversations and thorough consultations that had led to its creation.

When the COVID-19 pandemic broke out, Stacy was not sure that the INRJ was actually going to happen. She was frustrated and convinced that resistance was fueled by systemic racism and white fragility. She as well as the consultants who had helped create the model for the INRJ believed financial sustainability was well built into the model, and she thought that the anxiety that was finding its way into financial conversations was actually coming from fears of surrendering power and privilege. She also was worried that her frustrations were starting to get the best of her and that too much of the time she wasn't operating from her best self. She could feel space opening up between her and some of the lay leaders of the congregation.

And then the world changed. First came the pandemic. Then came the murder of George Floyd and continent-wide protests that seemed to be affecting change in a way that hadn't been seen before. Stacy decided that in her worship services, which were livestreamed and well attended online, she would go to a new level of frankness about colonialism, white privilege, and systemic racism, including the church's complicity. She braced herself for criticism—and got the opposite reaction. The feedback she received was positive and supportive. Church members expressed pride in the honesty of their leadership. Church leaders seemed to begin speaking of the INRJ in hopeful language again.

That is where we will have to leave the story. We are writing as the COVID-19 pandemic and the advance of Black Lives Matter and other initiatives for racial justice are still playing out. We can tell you that Stacy believes that two activities should guide her and Elm Avenue Church at this time: presencing and acts of solidarity with racialized neighbors. Stacy has a suspicion that the COVID-19 crisis is preparing the ground for deep presencing. Presencing requires going into a "field of unknowing," surrendering certainty over what we know, and refusing to engage in "downloading" old patterns of thinking and acting once again. The uncertainty of a world grasped by the coronavirus seems to be facilitating this entry into the field of unknowing. She's not yet certain how to prepare for the adaptive conversations that can enable presencing, but she and some lay leaders are working on it. She and others from Elm Avenue, along with partners from the mosques, Buddhist groups, synagogues, and Indigenous communities, are hitting the streets. With protective masks on their faces, they are taking a knee, marching, and singing. Sometimes the white marchers are strategically placing themselves between police and Blacks because they know that racialized people are more likely to be the first targets if the police turn to violence.

THE VIRTUE OF KENOSIS

As we sit with the powerful story of Elm Avenue Church and its web of partnerships, at this critical moment in their history, we believe this is the key question: How deeply will Elm Avenue engage in kenosis? *Kenosis* is a Greek word (found in the Second Testament) that implies self-emptying.[4] Theologically, it is associated with both Christ's incarnation and Christ's crucifixion. There is a traditional theological understanding that at the time of his incarnation, Christ (the Son, the Second Person of the Trinity) emptied himself of some of his attributes, including omniscience and omnipotence. God the Second Person becomes a servant. Within the passion, there is another emptying. Jesus empties himself of his power and fully accepts God's will. Over the centuries, there have been many theological debates about the concept of kenosis. It is not our desire to replicate those here. Instead, we want to speak about kenosis in the context of faith communities and how they thrive in the world today.

A faith community that thrives in today's world and truly serves God's mission, and is good for the world, has to go through periods of kenosis, of self-emptying. The ongoing dynamics in any congregation or parish—including organizational contingencies, power struggles, flawed and fickle human natures, the temptation to pride when we succeed and to bitterness when we fail—necessarily bring any faith community out of alignment with God's mission and out of harmony with its surrounding society. For alignment to happen with God's mission, with the Community of Heaven, and with society, kenosis has to occur. It is never easy. The release of tried-and-true beliefs and strategies in order to enter the field of unknowing is uncomfortable. Surrendering our wills to God's will requires humility. It will require the acceptance that we will be humiliated in the eyes of a world that worships success and a mainline church that is still addicted to measuring health in quantifiable ways. Reemerging from kenosis with a clear sense of mission may mean transforming a faith community in a way that will lead to the loss of members, money, and prestige. Such sacrifices are sometimes necessary in order to accept a form of vitality that cannot be quantified but can be measured only in terms of the transformation of hearts and the improvement of the lives of people who will never sit in a pew on a Sunday morning.

Over the last decade, Elm Avenue Church has been undergoing a certain self-emptying, giving up old assumptions about a church's leadership, mission, proper worship style, and more. What was becoming clear as the vision for the INRJ emerged was that the self-emptying would have to go much deeper. Initially, that seemed to be accepted, but what wasn't clear was the degree to which Elm Avenue's place in the world—like the place of the mainline church as a whole and the places of its privileged members—had been shaped by forces of colonialism. The self-emptying that was required of Elm Avenue now didn't just require giving up space in their building and the energy of ministers and volunteers together with financial resources. It also required giving up narrowness of vision and ignorance regarding systemic racism, white fragility, and the colonial project. When the actual depth of kenosis that would be required started to become clear, real resistance began to emerge. That resistance may well have taken hold. Certainly, Stacy was afraid that was going to happen. Then came the sweeping deconstructive moments of the COVID-19 crisis and the truth telling that followed George Floyd's murder. There is some feeling that these developments are acting as solvent on the resistance within Elm Avenue. We'll have to wait to see how deeply Elm Avenue will be able to enter into kenosis. We'll also have to wait to see how deeply the mainline church will embrace kenosis.

Of course, kenosis is not an end in itself. The surrender and self-emptying have value because they clear space for something else to appear. They create the possibility for something new, fresh, and even wonderful to emerge in the altered reality. But those things will not necessarily come unless there is a careful attending to the new reality and its possibilities. This is where Scharmer's concept of *presencing* is of value. Here is how he describes it: "Presencing, the blending of sensing and presence, means to connect from the Source of the highest future possibility and to bring it into the now. When moving into the state of presencing, perception begins to happen from a future possibility that depends on us to come into reality. In that state we step into our real being, who we really are, our authentic self. Presencing is a movement that lets us approach our self from the emerging future."[5]

After a faith community has been through a period of self-emptying —after assumed ways of thinking, acting, conversing, and being are surrendered—there can be an open space rife with possibility. Here, an encounter with something greater than ourselves becomes more possible. This thing greater than ourselves also is to be found in our deepest selves. Scharmer calls it "the Source" (evocatively capitalized) and the emerging future. Christians use terms like *the Spirit, the Divine, God, the Ground of Being* (Tillich's phrase). Scharmer tells the story of just such a deep encounter that happened to him when he was an adolescent. He was called out of school one day and taken to his family farm because of an emergency. As he approached the farm, he saw huge clouds of smoke. To his great shock, he realized that the whole farm where he had grown up was burning to the ground.

> As I watched my family's farmhouse burn, I began to feel that everything I thought I was, was gone—that was an example of sensing. When the boundary between the fire and me collapsed and I became aware that I wasn't separate from the fire and that the house that went up in flames wasn't separate from me—that was also sensing. In sensing, my perception originated in the current field: the burning fire right in front of me. But the next moment, when I felt elevated to another sphere of clarity and awareness and experienced a pull toward the source of silence and Self—that was foreshadowing of presencing.[6]

This description of a dramatic personal experience illustrates the shifts that a faith community (or any other group) can go through. Such shifts take us from the "normal" consciousness of everyday life (marked by rational thinking in which each person's awareness is located separately in his or her own head) to consciousness of the field (in this case not a fire, but the whole group, the whole community perhaps), and ultimately, to awareness of the Source. Reading Scharmer's description of his experience of the fire, seeing his use of words like "the source of silence and Self" (capitalized once again), one understands that he is conveying a quality of sacredness. This was a holy event for him. Similarly, faith communities who have surrendered to kenosis and entered into the deep encounter that Scharmer calls presencing speak of these times as blessed. There is a melting into deep whole-group communion in which God participates. In such experiences, which can last moments or months, we come to know things we didn't know before, and glimpses are offered of the future to which God calls us.

Stacy relates having many such experiences at Elm Avenue Church. Some lasted for brief moments, in worship or meditation groups or with away teams. Others lasted for many weeks, as in the "year of listening" with its sharing circles and Appreciative Inquiry. In Stacy's words, as well those of many commentators who looked for opportunities in the COVID-19 crisis, one can hear hope that the global pandemic, the rise of antiracist resistance, and other factors will serve as a kenosis for whole nations or even all of the world. Kenosis might help us know the whole human field better (sensing) and then be "elevated to another sphere of clarity," unveiling the Source and glimpses of a common future (presencing).

CONNECTING WITH EVERYTHING THAT ISN'T CHURCH

We have returned to the work of Scharmer in several chapters, and you may be wondering why we are giving so much attention to the work of a thinker who is not formally Christian or even writing within a religious framework. There are two reasons. First, Scharmer may be a management professional working outside formal religious structures, but it is easy to recognize his thinking as theological and to see how his worldview is resonant with the theology of the Community of Heaven and the analogy of spiritual mycelia that are saturated with the presence of the Divine. Second, Scharmer articulates a grammar for the descent into and the rising from the mycelia, without being restricted to the lexicon of any one faith tradition. This means he has given us a language that will enable a Christian faith community to share the sacred process of renewal through descent and reemergence with non-Christian and even nonreligious partner organizations. The interface between Elm Avenue Church and the INRJ is a good example of this. They have together arrived at a time in which they need to open up to a field of wisdom and knowing that is larger than any one partner, even all partners together. Scharmer's paradigm with its associated vocabulary could be one methodology for Elm Avenue to "go deep" with its partners without either betraying its way of being in faith or imposing that way on the partners.

This intersection between Christian churches and non-Christian communities and organizations is essential to attend to in this time and represents another kind of emptying out that we are witnessing in the thriving Christian communities we have been studying. Congregations like Grace Church (whose story we told in chapter 2) and University Street Church (whose story we told in chapter 4) have been moving from a primary relationship web made up of churches within their own denominations to relationship webs made up of diverse faith communities and non-faith-based organizations. It is a move from homogeneity to diversity. One leader in Elm Avenue Church captured the need for such a move in a great sentence: "The adaptive challenge of this church is to accommodate variety." It is a surrender of an old model in which denominations provide the principal container for their congregations. As those containers crumble, the congregations (and schools, camps, and other bodies) are poured out into the surrounding world, needing to form new primary relationships. This discharging process can feel like abandonment, but it may be the very liberation that is needed for revitalization.

Rebecca is a minister well aware of this particular kenosis as well as the essential task of attending to the interface between the congregation and partnerships with non-Christian bodies. She is also the one leader who spoke to us about Scharmer's work during our interviews. The congregation she serves, Parkway Church, has an interesting story. Parkway is located in a prosperous, semiurban community with many well-educated professionals. Several decades ago, it began to focus on offerings for youth and young adults and developed a breakthrough program called Horizons that became the center of the congregation's identity and the engine for growth. The growth was exponential. Relationships were sustained with youth as they moved into adulthood by providing them with opportunities to support and lead new generations entering into the Horizons programs. Adult social groups were shaped by connections made in Horizons. Three-quarters of the congregation were connected to it in some way.

Eventually, Horizons grew to be such a dominant part of Parkway's life that it became a great tree, casting a shadow over everything else happening in the congregation and making it difficult to find light and space for other ventures. A long-serving minister found a way to work in harmony with the lay staff who led Horizons, and there were many years of stability after the rapid growth of the congregation. When that minister retired, however, new ministers found themselves in conflict with the Horizons leaders and champions, struggling to clear some space for new kinds of growth.

Rebecca was invited to serve Parkway Church partly for her expertise in organizational change and conflict management. She quickly saw that "Horizons was not broken but was the thing that most needed repair." She felt that if the congregational system was going to shift in a way that would open space for new endeavors, a big vision would be required. Another different challenge at Parkway Church was also revealing itself, and Rebecca began to sense that this challenge might provide the context for the new "big vision." She could see that many people at Parkway were deeply concerned about the sociopolitical events shaping their nation. They wanted a way to connect their faith life to those realities. One might say that they were seeking a contemporary expression of the social gospel. Many were engaged in personal spiritual practices but didn't really know how to translate that into social action. There was a deep desire for the church to become more relevant in a troubled time.

Coincidentally (or providentially), Rebecca had been carrying an idea around in her back pocket for a number of years before coming to Parkway. She knew of an international organization that offers training programs designed to create change agents for a more just world. This organization is not itself faith based, but it holds values and practices highly compatible with Rebecca's understanding of the social gospel. Working with a network of colleges, this organization created schools for transformative leadership, shaping individuals and communities with skills for social innovation and change making. Rebecca's idea was to help birth the first of these schools set in a faith community. She felt that this idea could grow into the kind of "big vision" that could capture the imaginations of Parkway's members. She was right. The idea immediately caught fire and resonated throughout the congregation. Thinking strategically, Rebecca knew that the leadership school would have to be created in a way that did not engender competition with Horizons. So she first took her idea to the staff running the Horizons program. They liked it and were willing to reframe Horizons in harmony with it. The parents of the youth also liked it. A key aspect of the transformative leadership schools is action for change grounded in compassion. Worship was shaped to focus on Christian stories of compassion.

The plan to start with youth and grow from there really worked. As adults came on board, one could see an existential bridge being formed. Many of the Parkway congregation assumed that personal transformation would lead to social transformation, but they didn't know how to get there. Now they were being shown the way. A "lovely problem" emerged: so many people wanted to be involved with the new initiative that most had to be told to wait. Thinking about these developments, Rebecca reflected, "In my best moments of ministry, it feels like I'm in the current—that's how it feels now. There is a current that is carrying us along."

A wonderful array of opportunities and outcomes was carried on the current. Members of the Parkway congregation offered up hundreds of thousands of dollars to support the leadership school. A second campus was acquired and became the center of compassion-driven service to the homeless and others. A mighty circle of leaders in their twenties and thirties emerged to lead the church in new directions. A specialized professional in the congregation gave up her high-paying job to become a part-time staff person supporting the school and the mission ventures. New pastors from the millennial generation were hired. After the original year of partnership with the international organization ended, a group of lay leaders designed a bespoke curriculum to continue the leadership school. Parkway developed a network of interfaith partners.

Looking at this time of change at Parkway Church, we would *not* say it was experiencing a kenosis at that time. Yes, some things were being surrendered, like the old framing of the Horizons program, but it was actually more of a time of enrichment—of things flowing in and building up—rather than one of emptying out.

What is noteworthy, then, is that Parkway's kenosis came *on the heels of* this period of new growth and success. Checking in with Rebecca three years after our original contact, she reported, "We are in a year of being still. It is a year of suspending, of embracing an open will that allows us to turn to something new." She asked, "Are you familiar with Otto Scharmer's *Theory U?* For us, this is a year of presencing. It's scary in some ways. We are more sure of what is being let go than what is coming next." One thing Rebecca identified for letting go is the way Parkway Church has gathered for worship. She wasn't sure of new forms of liturgy, preaching, and ritual, but she knew they were needed. She could also look ahead and know that at some point, she would have to let go of her leadership: "My work is to get this church ready to be handed over to the leadership of millennials." We talked of the ways the kenosis prompted by the COVID-19 crisis might in turn provoke Parkway's transformation.

Notions of church growth that have been prevalent for decades might lead us to think that pausing for a year of being still means putting the brakes on growth or that surrendering to a form of kenosis and going into the unknown (as both Elm Avenue Church and Parkway Church are doing after periods of real success in pursuit of a new mission) mean abandoning a good thing. But there is a difference between losing ground and going to ground. This is a distinction between burying your head in the dirt while pretending that there are no problems on the one hand and diving into the mycelia in search of wisdom and nutrition on the other. One of the reasons we have chosen to celebrate the forms of growth embodied by Elm Avenue Church and Parkway Church is that they are both surrendering the neurotic attachment to perpetual, measurable growth. That neurosis has characterized Western society since the Enlightenment, leading to economies and spiritualities that are firmly embedded in an oppressive colonial project. It may be that the forms of surrender that these congregations embrace, with the grace to self-empty, will do more to counter the colonial project than the impressive mission projects that are being born in both faith communities.

Then again, kenosis and mission cannot be separated. They are qualities of the same life in faith, two moves in the same holy dance. This dance has a dangerous moment—the moment of success. At just that moment, there is a temptation to freeze the dance, to hold on to the success with tight hands. When we do this, we refuse the call to descent, and we refuse to be *turned inside out*. The most effective leaders and faith communities we encountered in our research were willing to be turned inside out over and over again. In fact, they embraced the turning and felt the power in it and the openness to Spirit. More than anything else perhaps, this capacity to be turned inside out—which is, after all, another way of describing a capacity for descent—is the right medicine for the death drive that has so many churches in its grasp.

QUESTIONS FOR DISCUSSION

1. The use of the term *kenosis* in this chapter is rooted in the Christian theological tradition, but it is taken in some new directions. What signs, if any, of kenosis, or self-emptying, have you seen in a faith community?

2. What might a process of self-emptying look like for your faith community?

3. Have you ever had an experience of "presencing," individually or as part of a group? What did that feel like?

TWO CHALLENGES

1. Learn about some aspects of the work of Otto Scharmer and his colleagues. His books, learning labs, and online courses are all available at https://www.ottoscharmer.com. See if anything resonates with your current life or faith community.

2. Lead a small group in a discussion of kenosis and what form of self-emptying might be appropriate for your faith community.

AFTERWORD
Supernova or Black Hole?

In the future, what will happen to your community of faith? Will you take hold of the future God is unfolding and let yourselves burn brightly and become a supernova? Or will you collapse inwardly and become a black hole, sucking energy, light, and life downward into nothingness?

Here's a story of a supernova church, a church that recognized the "forest fire" of its own impending demise, then embraced saying "yes!" to learning, leadership, risk, its own identity (even as it changed), and the gift of kenosis. The members of this church offered us this remarkable story of turning themselves inside out.

Northside Memorial Church is one of those grand, historic downtown churches that used to be full to overflowing on a Sunday morning. Most of its original congregation came from the same nineteenth-century immigrant community. The curving balcony of its sanctuary wraps itself around the upper level, bringing a second layer of congregants even closer to the pulpit, communion table, and choir loft. Built before electric amplification, the space is acoustically delightful, and it is a visual feast of lovingly handcrafted woodwork, from the pews and their carved floral ends to the inlaid walls. The sound of singing in that place was once hypnotic, beautiful, transporting. Northside Memorial was renowned for the harmonies lifted up by the jubilant singing of the people, for its massive Sunday school, and for its thunderous, powerful preachers. That church, as they say, was a living legend—back in the old days. Days now long past.

By the time Rob got to know this congregation, many years before we started researching this book, Northside Memorial Church was on its last legs. That's putting it generously. It was on the brink of collapse. Its coffers were empty. The deferred maintenance on the aging building was beyond daunting. The Sunday school was nonexistent. There was a complete absence of spiritual programming for adults, and there was only the smallest of struggling youth groups. Only a tiny handful of worshippers showed up on Sundays, and their singing was timid and distant. They spread themselves out thinly across the four-hundred-seat sanctuary, like seeds that had been scattered by a gust of wind. This congregation was at death's door. And then they had the audacity to call a new minister. It seemed unfair to them and to him to pretend that this congregation would even exist two years down the road.

If nothing else, God is the God of good surprises. A few years later, as we began the Thriving Christian Communities Project, Northside Memorial self-nominated themselves to us as a place worthy of study. It was hard to believe that they were still open, let alone had a story of thriving to tell. But now we were curious. On our visit, we discovered that Northside's building still needs some serious repairs. But the Sunday school has somehow come back to life. The finances have stabilized. Lay leadership is reinvigorated. New and diverse worshippers are starting to find their way into the sanctuary on Sundays. And the breadth of engagement with the wider community is truly astonishing—almost miraculous. They have traveled from the edge of the grave to being a fully thriving community once again.

THE TURNAROUND

How did all this transpire? The people of Northside Memorial tell the story like this. About fifteen years ago, said one, "We would have thirty people in the church service." They admitted that a few different ministers came and went over several years, but none stayed. One minister was "not a good fit at all and created a lot of..." This speaker faltered. "Turmoil," said another. The first speaker resumed, "Well, it was a disaster. It was a disaster as far as I was concerned. And so it was all kind of up in the air. . . . So when Terry [the current minister] arrived, (A) we were financially in serious trouble, and (B) there wasn't really a mission. There wasn't a focus."

A childcare center operated in the building, although it was not run by the Northside congregation. But that was the closest thing they could claim as something that served their community. "It was the raison d'être for this church for a very long while: Northside Daycare," we were told. Then the daycare center closed, and "that created quite a vacuum." Before long, the congregation began to speak of closing down for good. They were out of steam. They couldn't find the right ministers. Not many people were left even to *be* a church anymore. And the bills were piling up. The laypeople we interviewed talked about that dry, dire time: "There was a lot of intro-spection and searching of the community to say, 'What's our place? What's our place here?' We knew that somehow, we had to be involved in the com-munity." But no one knew how to do it. The gas tank was empty.

The congregation called a meeting—one final meeting to decide finally to close the doors. But someone suggested that they try again to "stay and grow" instead of "leave and die." A hesitant consensus in favor of the idea developed among the handful of folks attending the meet-ing. Some congregants were skeptical, wondering if that decision was an expression of denial, just putting off the inevitable—"a refusal to accept this wave of secularism that's going over us. . . . And it [the phrase 'stay and grow'] could be just words, right?"

They looked at each other for a few weeks, wondering what to do next. Then their minister gathered a few people together to do some learn-ing: "Terry [the minister] and a few of the people within the congrega-tion started reading about the missional church and basically joining God where God is working." They charged Terry with trying to make some community contacts. He called eighty community organizations to ask if Northside Memorial could help them in any way or partner with them on a project. Every agency said a firm "no." Terry relates the experience: "I said to our leaders, 'Look at where we are. Look at our location. We should be doing something. Surely there's someone who needs our space.' That's when I started calling around. No, no, no." Terry was on the brink of giving up and reporting back to the congregation that there wasn't much hope of making a community link. Then he got a phone call from the very first agency he had called. This time, a different agency staff person was on the line—she didn't know that he had called several days earlier. Here's how Terry describes what happened next:

> Once I gave up, the phone rang. They [the community agency] called
> me to see if I was willing to attend a meeting to start a daytime drop-in

center for street-identified men. And I said, "We've been looking for that." She asked, "Would you attend a meeting to help us find a location for the center?" I said, "No. Forget the meeting. Just do it here." So they did. That worked, and they were open here five days a week, but then they had to cut back to three because they weren't getting [their funding]. . . . And then finally they said, "Look, you know what? We're going to have to drop it altogether. Why doesn't Northside just take it on?" I didn't think it was going to work. I didn't think we'd ever get enough volunteers. And from Northside alone, we wouldn't have, but other people came in: the Christian Reform Church, university students, people from other congregations. . . . The drop-in was supposed to be six months' trial, but we never revisited it—it's just carried on for all this time.

Something really clicked after the drop-in got going in the Northside building. Some kind of invisible switch was thrown. We suspect it was the Holy Spirit at work. Other community agencies sat up and took notice. As one interviewee told us, "All of a sudden, then everybody knows what we're doing. Like I went to a meeting with all the stakeholders in the region who were running programs or doing things to help people who are homeless, and I said to a friend that it was almost embarrassing because well, you know, we're doing this little tiny thing and you know we're just muddling along, because none of us are professional at this, we're not trained social workers, any of us. We're muddling along, but the community does not see us that way. That was very complimentary."

New partnerships started to emerge. Conversation and reflection on their life as a faith community started to move from lament to hope. As one interviewee said, "It was a very deliberate introspective process that we went through and looked at everything from our structures to what our demographic was and to make a decision to say, 'We're going to stay and grow.'"

Finances were still a serious problem. At one point, the treasurer "basically stood up and . . . he laid it on the line. 'Look, based on our current burn rate we have eight months.' And that was, you know, that was after we had started developing all those other [initiatives with community partners]." But the congregation was not scared off. They had decided to go for it, blow it all out, and not hold back. They were going full super-nova. A stewardship campaign, the first in several years, completely defied expectations, with financial pledges and giving increasing by more than 15 percent. A new outreach project received an additional $20,000 in gifts. The generosity, energy, and transformation of the congregation took on new, unplanned forms:

> *Then people were donating clothes and small household items for people who needed them. . . . Out of the drop-in center, we started to get people coming into the church service, which was a tremendous learning experience. We had one person who would just interrupt the minister. Stand up and talk to the minister during the sermon. Or, if Terry had good news she would get up and spill, and Terry would try to stop her, and you couldn't. We have another person who's very mentally ill and addicted, but he's a gifted musician. So he would come in and play. The first time, he came in, and he sat, and he got up, and he sat, and he got up, and then when it came time for his turn to play, he was nowhere to be found. Next time he came in and stayed for a little bit longer. But now he's a regular part of our service.*

More and more street-identified people came in, with all the challenges and blessings they brought with them. The initial discomfort for the comfortable middle-class people of Northside Memorial gave way to a readiness to welcome and include all comers. They knew that the only other alternative was one they had already faced, up close: the death of their church.

A FLOOD OF LIGHT AND ENERGY

More and more, laypeople stepped up and brought their skills to the leadership needs that had gone unmet for several years. One person said, "My dad was sick, and he eventually died, and I was a partner in a struggling company. So I just didn't have the personal energy. So, you know, the stars aligned, and I was looking for an opportunity. So Terry contacted me, and we had a lot of conversations about missional church. I said, 'You know, I'm looking for something that I can develop a passion for. But keeping the doors open on an old building doesn't really excite me.' . . . Then we started talking about missional church. And then I got more and more excited." The missional impulse kept rippling outward. The interview group's stories just tumbled out one after another:

> Then we asked the chaplain at the [local prison] to bring four inmates to tell their story. People were just bawling their eyes out. . . . We worshiped at the hospital. . . . There was the group that was interested in working with the homeless and marginally housed. There was one working for prisoners. There was one that wanted to focus on music. . . . Another group connected to hospital care. . . . I'm involved in Toastmasters and a few other groups, so I got a bunch of friends to help, and they were facilitators in some of the bigger groups. . . . We brought in Judge _____, who you see in the paper [to tell us about his work in the justice system]. . . . Now we've got . . . people from a bunch of different faiths, and we've got people who grew up outside of the church.

For Northside Memorial, it's been full-on supernova ever since. The effects of their faithful choice to serve others extend well beyond their membership: "Over half the volunteers [in our outreach projects] are from outside of the congregation now. It's too big to stop. . . . It's like giving birth to a child. I mean, you give birth, you let them grow, and you send them off into the world. . . . It's really all about integrity. The matching of what you talk about on Sunday and what you do during the week. . . . We are constantly examining ourselves for who we really are. Constantly. And that comes from . . . our struggle [to survive]."

Another person chimed in right away: "We went to the precipice, and we still are there . . . but spiritually we're really healthy—it's the building that's horrible. . . . I always joke that I want our logo to be 'We might not be good looking, but we're looking good.'"

Service to the community has redefined Northside in ways they never expected. They were inward looking, sad, and collapsing in on themselves like a black hole that uses up resources without sharing any light. But the turn outward radically shifted the congregation. The laypeople of Northside now have a keen sense of being on mission together with God: "I think the other thing is once you start working—thinking in that outreach mode, it's no longer about this building and that sanctuary. It's more about just joining God." They keep their expectations modest: "We're not counting on being a big church in worship [numbers]. . . . You can't have your ego attached to any of it. Because it's not about us in any way; it's about truly developing community where none existed. And that comes in many, many, many forms. . . . But last year, we had the best financial year that we've had in probably fifteen years."

What's happening at Northside these days? Their choice to go supernova (our term, not theirs) has prompted all manner of flourishing ministry and life. They are still financially strapped. Their building still needs significant repairs. But they are thriving in every possible way. This is just a sample of their activities and life together since they made the decision not to give up:

- sharing their sanctuary with other faith groups

- formally and publicly welcoming LGBTQ+ persons, including an equal marriage policy

- organizing weekly "Bible and Beers" in a local pub

- fully renovating, then owning and operating a house for women recovering from addictions

- sponsoring refugees jointly with a secular community association

- renovating the kitchen to serve community groups as well as church needs

- housing a community medical clinic

- hosting a preschool

- being a distribution point for the city's large food bank network

- providing afterschool programming for Syrian refugees

- renting classrooms for ESL (English as a second language) training

None of this existed before the fateful meeting at which they planned to close the church. Supernovas are like that: they explode and burn more brightly than ever.

One last moving story from Northside Memorial. Someone approached them about a local homeless man who had to cart around his belongings all day and was having trouble managing. Although Northside does not have a shelter, they do have a parking lot. The idea was hatched to build lockers in the parking lot for homeless people to store their few possessions. Terry, the minister, describes how things went from there:

> So then Daniel comes along. He doesn't talk to anybody. And this isn't a place for him to stay, so I'm still not sure where he sleeps through the winter or anything . . . but now his stuff is here [in one of the lockers in the parking lot], and he has a key. And they said it would have brought tears to your eyes when they gave him the key. He looked at it and said, "I've never had a key to anything." . . . He comes and goes. At one time, somebody suggested we move the locker over so he's out of the way when the preschool's coming out, and people won't be bothered by him. . . . I said, "No." People need to know when they come to Northside, it's that kind of place, and he is not dangerous.

THE END?

As we come to the end of the Thriving Christian Communities Project—at least this part of it—some of our starting assumptions remain with us and indeed have been strengthened through our encounters with these amazing communities of faith. We assumed, and now we can firmly attest, that the good work of our gracious God is unstoppable. Even when the mainline church declines as a total body, God is still at work in the world. That divine movement can be discerned if we stop to notice and take off our blinders.

We'll leave you with our parting thoughts about the future. Three options lie ahead for Christian communities in the mainline tradition: *red dwarf star*, *black hole*, or *supernova*.

Some (perhaps many) mainline congregations will die a quiet, slow, dignified death. Inertia will take over, and they will become red dwarf stars. As ministers and fellow Christians, we are sincerely grateful for their history of service, sacrifice, worship, and witness. We give God thanks for them, and we're not here to shame them. But their collapse and contraction are already underway. Congregations and parishes like this can't do anything more than be their own shrinking selves, and then the end will come.

Some congregations will become black holes, sucking in resources of time, money, and energy without giving much in return to the universe around them. They've lost a missional focus, and they express the vices of greed, narcissism, and survivalism more than the virtues we've described in this book. Doing nothing or the same old ineffective things will lead inevitably to a faith community becoming a black hole, draining life and energy, becoming invisible, and sharing no light. Those places make us sad, and we hope there will not be many like this.

But a few Christian communities (maybe yours?) will become supernovas. They will trust wherever the Spirit leads them—out into the community, off the page into the unknown and unwritten—always drawing them outward and making them ever more radiant in Christ. They will pour themselves out, throwing fire and light into greater and wider orbits, drawing in neighbors and connecting with partners, shining brighter and brighter as the years go by. They will give themselves fully to the mission of God, say "yes!" over and over, keep learning, embrace leadership, take courageous risks, stay rooted in their (evolving) identity, surrender to the Divine purposes, and turn themselves inside out for the greater good of the communities around them and the wider world. They will exist for the reason the Holy Spirit first called the church into being: to serve the world God loves.

Supernovas don't last forever either.

But what a way to go.

*

APPENDIX 1

QUESTIONS ASKED AT INTERVIEWS WITH THRIVING CHRISTIAN COMMUNITIES

OPEN-ENDED BEGINNING QUESTIONS

1. What is the most important thing one needs to know about your faith community to understand it? Name a second thing. Perhaps a third.

2. What makes your faith community vital or thriving?

3. What biblical story or image best represents or describes this ministry/community for you?

4. What is the generational and demographic character of this ministry/community?

QUESTIONS ABOUT CONTEXT

1. Please describe the wider context or community in which this ministry is happening?

2. How does this ministry/community relate to or witness to the Christian faith in that wider context?

3. Consider the theological and spiritual foundations of your ministry or faith community. How are these connected to the realities and needs of the larger context in which you find yourself?

4. How does this ministry/faith community relate to other faith communities?

QUESTIONS ABOUT THE LEADERSHIP AND ACTIVITIES OF THE FAITH COMMUNITY

1. How would you describe the leadership of this ministry or community?

2. What forms of in-community leadership training are available if any?

3. How is the good news about God and the Christian faith shared in or through this ministry?

4. Are people in your faith community engaging in particular spiritual practices? Identify those practices and what this engagement seems to be producing.

5. How do people here learn about the Christian faith?

6. How do people connected with this ministry take part in justice making, peace seeking, and/or environmental causes?

7. What would you say is the role of small groups (three to twelve persons) in this ministry?

QUESTIONS ABOUT PERSONAL INVOLVEMENT AND FINAL REFLECTIONS

1. How did you become involved in this community/ministry?

2. How is your personal faith shaped or influenced by taking part in this ministry?

3. How have things changed here since you became involved?

4. What is the bravest thing you have done in this ministry?

5. Is there anything else you'd like to tell us about your faith community?

APPENDIX 2

A FOUR-WEEK STUDY AND DISCUSSION PROCESS
Exploring Descent, Renewal, and Reemergence

This four-week process is intended to help a faith community attend to the move into *depth*. This is all about dropping down into the mycelia and the root system of a faith community to find intelligence and nutrients, opening to and embracing the agency of the Divine, moving from a closed system to an open system, and uncovering the various ways in which the community is saying "no!" and "yes!" to God's call and leading so that it can surrender the former and nurture the latter.

After facilitating the process for four weeks, you will have enough experience with it that you will be able to continue on, if you wish, generating your own design for weeks five, six, and beyond.

GETTING STARTED

To begin, gather a group of six to twelve people from the faith community who will commit to spending ninety minutes together each week and to giving some time to spiritual practices on each day between sessions. The first time you do this, form the group by personal invitation. Don't just advertise it in the church newsletter or website and wait to see who comes. You want a group of committed individuals who will follow through all four sessions, who are capable of attentive listening to other group members, and who can articulate their hopes, fears, and emotions in a respectful and insightful way.

PREPARING THE SPACE

Each week before the group gathers, take some time to prepare the room. Tidy it. Attend to the layout of the whole room, giving it some coherence and aesthetic appeal. Bring in visual art to set the tone. Set the chairs in a circle and have a candle on a table in the middle.

PROCESS FOR EACH WEEKLY SESSION

When the group gathers, move through these stages:

- *Opening.* Light the candle and do a quick check-in.

- *Spiritual practice.* Say a prayer, read a portion of the Bible, and engage in a few minutes of contemplative prayer or mindfulness practice.

- *Sharing circle.* Encourage folks to speak from the heart and to be honest.

- *Wrap up.* Suggest spiritual practices for the coming week and offer a closing prayer.

Here are some suggestions for each stage. Feel free to adjust according to your own experience and your intuition regarding what the group needs.

Opening

- After you have lit the candle, go around the circle and have each person offer a word on how they are doing or how their week has been.

- It is important to set the norm that each person only has about one minute to do this, or you'll find that this stage takes up too much time.

- You can simply ask, "How was your week?" Or you can be a little more directive by inviting each person to offer one "apple" and one "onion" from the week, or one moment of light and one moment of shadow.

Spiritual Practice

- The prayer can be spontaneous or one that you know and like.

- As a suggestion, the prayer attributed to Saint Francis works well and sets the tone for speaking and listening in the next stage:

  Lord, make me an instrument of your peace:
  where there is hatred, let me sow love;
  where there is injury, pardon;
  where there is doubt, faith;
  where there is despair, hope;
  where there is darkness, light;
  where there is sadness, joy.
  O God, grant that I may not so much seek
  to be consoled as to console,
  to be understood as to understand,
  to be loved as to love.
  For it is in giving that we receive,
  it is in pardoning that we are pardoned,
  and it is in dying that we are born to eternal life.
  Amen.

- Suggestions for each week's Bible reading are below.

- A helpful contemplative practice is to invite participants to close their eyes and take about two minutes to allow images of people in their faith community to float before their eyes. Tell them just to let this happen. It's not necessary to force images or to evaluate the ones that come. Then spend about five minutes repeating the following loving-kindness prayer. It is a blessing upon those whom they have imagined. You can say it out loud and have folks repeat it silently in their minds. After a few minutes, you can also fall silent because they will have memorized it.

May you feel protected and safe.
May you feel contented and pleased.
May your bodies support you with strength.
May your lives unfold in God's grace.

Sharing Circle

In a sharing circle, a question is asked, then the group goes around the circle, giving each person a chance to answer the question. Listed below are the norms that should be followed in a sharing circle. We suggest that you make the effort to have the group really adopt and adhere to the norms. Depending on your space and so forth, you may wish to display them prominently on a large screen, posters, or a handout.

- Listen carefully, generously, and with an open spirit.

- Don't interrupt.

- Don't rehearse your own offering while others are speaking.

- Speak in a way that opens to possibility rather than closing down into pessimism, even when speaking from a place of fear, anxiety, anger, or pain.

- Allow room for faith and hope.

- Be mindful of time.

- Feel free to pass.

- Honor confidentiality.

- Remember, the most important voice in this conversation is the Spirit. Listen for it!

The use of a talking stick or a similar object helps. One only speaks when holding the stick. If people speak just briefly and there is time remaining, you might want to go around the circle a second or even a third time. Sometimes the good stuff (or the *real* stuff) comes up in these rounds.

Wrap Up

- Ask people to give five or ten minutes each day until the next session to continue the process on their own.

- Doing the loving-kindness prayer is a good practice. So is simply praying in one's own way for the faith community.

- If they wish, folks can continue to engage with the sharing circle questions in a journal. They can report back during the check-in next week.

- Offer a simple prayer, perhaps attending to things heard in the sharing circle.

- You may wish to provide a take-home handout reminding them of the practices noted above or others you may suggest for each week.

CONTENT FOR THE FIRST FOUR WEEKS

Week One

- Read Matthew 5:1–16. It sets a tone of blessing in weakness and calls out our light and salt.

- Take a good amount of time to go over and establish the sharing circle norms.

- Here is a good question for this round: "What are your hopes and fears for our faith community?" You might have to do two or three rounds to get the conversation really going.

- If someone is not adhering to the norms or talking too long, you might need to do a gentle intervention with that person after the session so that this doesn't happen the following week.

- Encourage people to engage in spiritual practice during the week. They may choose the loving-kindness prayer or journaling. They might also choose some kind of practice they already do, such as mindfulness meditation or meditative walking.

Week Two

- Read Revelation 1:1-11 and Revelation 2:1-17. Say a little bit about how each church has an "angel"—a collective personality or a group spirit—and how the work that the group is doing over these weeks is about calling out the best parts of that angel: its hope, its honesty, its courage, its mission, and so forth. If you want to do a little research and thinking about this before the session, look up "Walter Wink angel of the church" online. You will find Wink's work on this evocative. If you really want to dive in, read his "Powers" trilogy (see details in the bibliography).

- A good practice following this reading is to ask people to close their eyes, allow glimpses of the faith community's angel to float through their minds, and then repeat the loving-kindness prayer for several minutes.

- Here is a good question for the sharing circle: "What are the traits of this faith community's angel? What are its strengths, its fears, its hopes, its hang-ups? What makes it joyous? What makes it angry?"

- Again, encourage people to engage in spiritual practice during the week. They might want to journal about the angel or even draw, paint, or sculpt it.

Week Three

- Print out excerpts from the book of Jonah and ask people around the circle to read them (Jonah 1:1-5, 15-17; 2:8-10; 3:1-5, 10; 4:1-4). Fill in the story between excerpts so that the sweep of the whole story is covered. Alternatively, have a member of the group retell Jonah's story from memory.

- Do the loving-kindness exercise again, or just ask people to sit in silence focusing on their breath as a mindfulness practice. Invite the Spirit to be in the breath.

- Here is a question for the sharing circle: "At times, Jonah accepted God's call and lived out his mission. At other times, he fled from the call and abandoned the mission. In what ways are we in this faith community accepting and fleeing from our call and our mission?"

- Again, encourage people to engage in spiritual practice during the week.

Week Four

- Read Luke 4:16–21.

- This time, ask participants to close their eyes and allow images of people in the larger community and world to float before them. Do this for a couple of minutes, then spend five minutes in loving-kindness prayer directed toward those people. Folks might want to offer prayer for a specific person or for all those who came to mind.

- Here are some questions for the sharing circle: "What is this faith community's mission in our context? What do we need to embrace for that mission to grow? What do we need to stop doing for that mission to grow? How do we need to become vulnerable for that mission to grow?" You might want to pose some of these questions in round one and others in round two.

- End with a discussion of how folks see their lives and their church differently after these four weeks. What are they going to do for spiritual practice after these sessions have ended?

WHAT NEXT?

Decide together if the group wishes to continue to meet in this way or to invite additional participants. If you do, carry on. If this is not feasible or desired at this point, suggest members commit to meditating on and praying over what has happened in the four weeks together, listening carefully for the Spirit's guidance as to where the community is being led, how to begin, and so forth. Set a date to come back together (perhaps in a month) to share insights and ask together, "What next?"

NOTES

INTRODUCTION

1 We use the terms *mainline church* and *liberal church* interchangeably in this volume. Neither is an ideal descriptor of the branch of Protestant Christianity to which we refer. The *mainline church* is a broad term that covers denominations such as most Presbyterians, Methodists, Lutherans, United Churches, Disciples, Anglicans, the Episcopal tradition, and some Baptists—among others. For much of the twentieth century, these bodies made up "mainline Protestantism" in distinction to evangelical Christianity and Pentecostal or charismatic churches. There was a time in Canada and the United States when the "mainline" did occupy the cultural mainstream and significantly overshadowed evangelicals and charismatics in terms of numbers. That time is long past.

2 See appendix I for the questions that guided the interviews.

CHAPTER 1

1 "Jack pine and lodgepole pine have serotinous cones (protected by a waxy coating) that require the heat of fire to release their seeds. Fire also produces favourable conditions for the seeds of these pines to germinate. Nutrients are released in the soil, mineral soil is exposed, competing species are eliminated and the amount of sunlight on the forest floor is increased. Both jack and lodgepole pine depend on fire to regenerate." "Fire Ecology," Natural Resources Canada, July 7, 2020, https://tinyurl.com/3he4p4b6. If the church today is experiencing a forest fire, what new seeds are we willing to disperse so that new life can flourish?

2 By "Community of Heaven," we mean what has traditionally been called the "Kingdom of Heaven." We prefer this term because it intentionally loses resonance with the patriarchy and domination of "kingdom." *Community* says something different about power relations and the strength of mutual

connection and interdependence. See chapter 4, "Openhearted Leadership," for a broader elaboration of this.

3   Sigmund Freud, *Beyond the Pleasure Principle*, International Psycho-analytical Library 4, ed. Ernest Jones, trans. C. J. M. Hubback (London: International Psycho-analytical Press, 1922).

4   See, for example, Reginald W. Bibby, *Fragmented Gods: The Poverty and Potential of Religion in Canada* (Toronto: Stoddart, 1987); Reginald W. Bibby, *Unknown Gods: The Ongoing Story of Religion in Canada* (Toronto: Stoddart, 1993); Reginald W. Bibby, *Restless Gods: The Renaissance of Religion in Canada* (Toronto: Novalis, 2004); and Reginald W. Bibby, *Resilient Gods: Being Pro-religious, Low Religious, or No Religious in Canada* (Vancouver: University of British Columbia Press, 2017).

5   Edward F. Kelly, Adam Crabtree, and Paul Marshall, eds., *Beyond Physicalism: Toward Reconciliation of Science and Spirituality* (London: Rowman & Littlefield, 2015), vii.

6   See Brad Christerson and Richard Flory, *The Rise of Network Christianity: How Independent Leaders Are Changing the Religious Landscape* (New York: Oxford University Press, 2017). Christerson and Flory argue that independently networked churches represent the only branch of Christianity in North America that is growing faster than the general population.

7   Fetishization in its use here, according to Merriam-Webster, is to regard something with "extravagant irrational devotion." *Merriam-Webster*, s.v. "fetishism (n.)," accessed March 29, 2021, https://www.merriam-webster.com/dictionary/fetishism.

CHAPTER 2

1   We favor the terms *First Testament* and *Second Testament* rather than the conventional *Old Testament* and *New Testament* as a way to avoid the implication that the Christian authors' witness is inevitably *better* because it is *newer*.

2   For a complete study of Wink's treatment of "the Powers," see Walter Wink, *Naming the Powers: The Language of Power in the New Testament* (Minneapolis: Augsburg Fortress, 1983); Walter Wink, *Unmasking the Powers: The Invisible Forces That Determine Human Existence* (Minneapolis: Augsburg Fortress, 1986); and Walter Wink, *Engaging the Powers: Discernment and Resistance in a World of Domination* (Minneapolis: Fortress, 1992). For an overview, see Walter Wink, *Transforming the Powers: Peace, Justice, and the Domination System* (Minneapolis: Fortress, 2006).

3   Edwin H. Friedman, *Friedman's Fables* (New York: Guilford, 1990), "The Failure of Syntax," Kindle.

4   Edwin H. Friedman, *Generation to Generation: Family Process in Church and Synagogue* (New York: Guilford, 2011); Edwin H. Friedman, *A Failure of Nerve: Leadership in the Age of the Quick Fix*, ed. Margaret M. Treadwell and Edward W. Beal (New York: Church Publishing, 1999).

5   Otto Scharmer and Katrin Kaeufer, *Leading from the Emerging Future: From Ego-system to Eco-system Economies* (San Francisco: Berrett-Koehler, 2013); Otto Scharmer, *Theory U: Leading from the Future as It Emerges*, 2nd ed. (Oakland, CA: Berrett-Koehler, 2016).

6   Walter Wink, *Transforming Bible Study: A Leader's Guide*, rev. ed. (Eugene, OR: Wipf & Stock, 2009).

7   Gil Rendle and Alice Mann, *Holy Conversations: Strategic Planning as a Spiritual Practice for Congregations* (Lanham, MD: Rowman & Littlefield, 2003).

8   Martha Grace Reese, *Unbinding the Gospel: Real Life Evangelism*, 2nd ed. (Nashville: Chalice, 2009).

9   Walter Wink, *The Powers That Be: Theology for a New Millennium* (New York: Doubleday, 1999).

CHAPTER 3

1   William Barclay, *The Gospel of John*, vol. 2, Daily Study Bible Series, rev. ed. (Philadelphia: Westminster, 1975), 20.

2   James Russell Lowell, "The Present Crisis" (1845), public domain, accessed March 29, 2021, https://poets.org/poem/present-crisis.

3   "America's Changing Religious Landscape," Pew Research Center, May 12, 2015, https://tinyurl.com/fn5daubk.

4   Christine Jerrett, "The Changing Shape of the Church," *Reflections on Being the Church in God's New Creation* (blog), September 29, 2015, https://tinyurl.com/368h8zwd.

5   Margaret Wheatley, *Who Do We Choose to Be? Facing Reality, Claiming Leadership, Restoring Sanity* (Oakland, CA: Berrett-Koehler, 2017), 28.

6   From an unpublished address first offered by this minister at a conference in 2016 and shared in an email to the authors and used with permission.

7   "Deep change or slow death" were the only two options available to Asbury United Methodist Church in Austin, Texas, before it chose radical transformation. Read more about them in Eileen E. Flynn's article, "A Dying Texas Church Gives Life to a New Congregation," *Faith and Leadership*, April 4, 2017, https://tinyurl.com/2f9dkcjj.

CHAPTER 4

1 *Ground of Being* as a term for God was a favorite expression of Paul Tillich, a German American theologian who tried to break away from traditional theism. See his multivolume *Systematic Theology*, 3 vols. (Chicago: University of Chicago Press, 1951–63).

2 Eric McLuhan, introduction to *The Medium and the Light: Reflections on Religion*, by Marshall McLuhan, ed. Eric McLuhan and Jacek Szklarek (Toronto: Stoddart, 1999), xv.

3 McLuhan, xvi–xvii.

4 Scharmer and Kaeufer, *Leading from the Emerging Future*, 18.

5 Otto Scharmer, *Addressing the Blind Spot of Our Time: An Executive Summary of the New Book by Otto Scharmer—"Theory U: Leading from the Future as It Emerges"* (Cambridge, MA: Society for Organizational Learning North America, 2016), 1, https://tinyurl.com/ya4587tr.

6 Scharmer, *Theory U*, 18.

7 Otto Scharmer, "The U: One Process, Five Movements," Presencing Institute, accessed March 29, 2021, https://tinyurl.com/8a6pv6mx.

8 See chapter 2, "Starting with 'Yes!,'" for a detailed description of adaptive conversations.

CHAPTER 5

1 Harry Emerson Fosdick, "God of Grace and God of Glory" (1930), public domain, accessed March 29, 2021, https://hymnary.org/text/god_of_grace _and_god_of_glory.

2 C. Michael Hawn, "History of Hymns: 'God of Grace and God of Glory,'" Discipleship Ministries: United Methodist Church, June 20, 2013, https://tinyurl .com/eucx6afy.

3 This refrain echoes across many parts of the First Testament (Old Testament). See also Deut 31:6–7, 23; Judg 1:6; 1 Chr 28:20; Pss 27:14, 31:24.

4 Wheatley, *Who Do We Choose to Be?*, 25.

5 Wheatley, 32.

CHAPTER 6

1 John A. Shedd, "Salt from My Attic [1928]," cited in Fred R. Shapiro, ed., *The Yale Book of Quotations* (New Haven, CT: Yale University Press, 2006), 705.

2 Christine Jerrett, "Cultivating Congregations" (unpublished presentation, Cruxifusion Conference, Brampton, ON, April 2016).

3   Wheatley, *Who Do We Choose to Be?*, 202.
4   John Bell, "Episode 8," in *Illumin8faith*, podcast, September 15, 2016, https://tinyurl.com/2ax6zuwt.

CHAPTER 7

1   Learn more about Appreciative Inquiry here: "Introduction to Appreciative Inquiry," AI Commons, accessed March 29, 2021, https://tinyurl.com/2car9srv.
2   Scharmer, *Theory U*, 161.
3   See chapter 2, "Starting with 'Yes!,'" for a detailed description of adaptive conversations.
4   Christ "emptied [Greek: *ekenoōsen > kenoō*, 'to empty'; 'to make empty'] himself, taking the form of a slave, being born in human likeness. And being found in human form, he humbled himself and became obedient to the point of death—even death on a cross" (Phil 2:7–8).
5   Scharmer, *Theory U*, 161.
6   Scharmer, 161.

BIBLIOGRAPHY

Barclay, William. *The Gospel of John*. Vol. 2. Daily Study Bible Series. Rev. ed. Philadelphia: Westminster, 1975.

Bell, John. "Episode 8." In *Illumin8faith*, podcast, September 15, 2016. https://tinyurl.com/2ax6zuwt.

Bibby, Reginald W. *Fragmented Gods: The Poverty and Potential of Religion in Canada*. Toronto: Stoddart, 1987.

——. *Resilient Gods: Being Pro-religious, Low Religious, or No Religious in Canada*. Vancouver: University of British Columbia Press, 2017.

——. *Restless Gods: The Renaissance of Religion in Canada*. Toronto: Novalis, 2004.

——. *Unknown Gods: The Ongoing Story of Religion in Canada*. Toronto: Stoddart, 1993.

Christerson, Brad, and Richard Flory. *The Rise of Network Christianity: How Independent Leaders Are Changing the Religious Landscape*. New York: Oxford University Press, 2017.

Flynn, Eileen E. "A Dying Texas Church Gives Life to a New Congregation." *Faith and Leadership*, April 4, 2017. https://tinyurl.com/2f9dkcjj.

Fosdick, Harry Emerson. "God of Grace and God of Glory." Public domain, 1930. Accessed March 29, 2021. https://hymnary.org/text/god_of_grace_and_god_of_glory.

Freud, Sigmund. *Beyond the Pleasure Principle*. International Psycho-analytical Library 4. Edited by Ernest Jones. Translated by C. J. M. Hubback. London: International Psycho-analytical Press, 1922.

Friedman, Edwin H. *A Failure of Nerve: Leadership in the Age of the Quick Fix*. Edited by Margaret M. Treadwell and Edward W. Beal. New York: Church Publishing, 1999.

——. *Friedman's Fables*. New York: Guilford, 1990.

——. *Generation to Generation: Family Process in Church and Synagogue*. New York: Guilford, 2011.

Hawn, C. Michael. "History of Hymns: 'God of Grace and God of Glory.'" Discipleship Ministries: The United Methodist Church, June 20, 2013. https://tinyurl.com/eucx6afy.

Jerrett, Christine. "The Changing Shape of the Church." *Reflections on Being the Church in God's New Creation* (blog), September 29, 2015. https://tinyurl.com/368h8zwd.

———. "Cultivating Congregations." Unpublished presentation at the Cruxifusion Conference, Brampton, ON, April 2016.

Kelly, Edward F., Adam Crabtree, and Paul Marshall, eds. *Beyond Physicalism: Toward Reconciliation of Science and Spirituality.* London: Rowman & Littlefield, 2015.

Lowell, James Russell. "The Present Crisis." Public domain, 1845. Accessed March 29, 2021. https://poets.org/poem/present-crisis.

McLuhan, Marshall. *The Medium and the Light: Reflections on Religion.* Toronto: Stoddart, 1999.

Reese, Martha Grace. *Unbinding the Gospel: Real Life Evangelism.* 2nd ed. Nashville, TN: Chalice, 2009.

Rendle, Gil, and Alice Mann. *Holy Conversations: Strategic Planning as a Spiritual Practice for Congregations.* Lanham, MD: Rowman & Littlefield, 2003.

Scharmer, Otto. *Addressing the Blind Spot of Our Time: An Executive Summary of of the New Book by Otto Scharmer—"Theory U: Leading from the Future as It Emerges."* Cambridge, MA: Society for Organizational Learning North America, 2016. https://tinyurl.com/ya4587tr.

———. *Theory U: Leading from the Future as It Emerges.* 2nd ed. Oakland, CA: Berrett-Koehler, 2016.

———. "The U: One Process, Five Movements." Presencing Institute. Accessed March 29, 2021. https://tinyurl.com/8a6pv6mx.

Scharmer, Otto, and Katrin Kaeufer. *Leading from the Emerging Future.* San Francisco, CA: Berrett-Koehler, 2013.

Shedd, John A. "Salt from My Attic [1928]." In *The Yale Book of Quotations,* edited by Fred R. Shapiro, 705. New Haven, CT: Yale University Press, 2006.

Tillich, Paul. Systematic Theology. 3 vols. Chicago: University of Chicago Press, 1951–1963.

Wheatley, Margaret. *Who Do We Choose to Be? Facing Reality, Claiming Leadership, Restoring Sanity.* Oakland, CA: Berrett-Koehler, 2017.

Wink, Walter. *Engaging the Powers: Discernment and Resistance in a World of Domination.* Minneapolis: Fortress, 1992.

———. *Naming the Powers: The Language of Power in the New Testament.* Minneapolis: Augsburg Fortress, 1983.

———. *The Powers That Be: Theology for a New Millennium.* New York: Doubleday, 1999.

———. *Transforming Bible Study: A Leader's Guide.* Rev. ed. Eugene, OR: Wipf & Stock, 2009.

———. *Transforming the Powers: Peace, Justice, and the Domination System.* Minneapolis: Fortress, 2006.

———. *Unmasking the Powers: The Invisible Forces That Determine Human Existence.* Minneapolis: Augsburg Fortress, 1986.